THE GREAT BRITISH
BAKE OFF
Another Slice

THE TIERS, THE TRIUMPHS AND THE TENT

A SHOW-STOPPING SELECTION OF
YOUR FAVOURITE *BAKE OFF* MOMENTS

First published in Great Britain in 2015 by Hodder & Stoughton
An Hachette UK company

1

A CIP catalogue record for this title is available from the British Library

Hardback ISBN 978 1 473 61560 1
Ebook ISBN 978 1 473 61561 8

Authors: Andy Baker, Andrew Webb
Editorial Director: Nicky Ross
Editor: Briony Gowlett
Executive Editor: Sharon Powers
Consultant Editor: Jo Bunting
Project Editor: Patricia Burgess
Art Director: Mark Read
Designer: Estuary English
Illustrations: Melvyn Evans

With special thanks to Anna Beattie, Rupert Frisby, Julia Henderson, and Stuart Cooper.

Typeset in Whitney, Caslon, Mostra and Knockout

Printed and bound in Germany by Mohn media

Hodder & Stoughton policy is to use papers that are natural, renewable and recyclable products and made from wood grown in sustainable forests. The logging and manufacturing processes are expected to conform to the environmental regulations of the country of origin.

Hodder & Stoughton Ltd
Carmelite House
50 Victoria Embankment
London EC4Y 0DZ

www.hodder.co.uk

HELLO *Bake Off* FANS!

IT'S BEEN SIX years since the snowy white turrets of the *Bake Off* tent first put in an appearance. Inside, rows of spotless worktops, pristine utensils, gleaming jars of ingredients, and, above all, a sense of stillness and calm. Then arrived a buoyant Mel and Sue, closely followed by Mary, Paul and a whole host of amazing bakers, and it's been a flour-sugar-and-egg-based riot ever since.

We've had Signatures that made bakers sob, Technicals that no one had heard of (schichttorte, anyone?), and Showstoppers – boy, have we had Showstoppers. A magnificent lion's head made out of bread, a George & dragon biscuit creation and even the Moulin Rouge in cake. The creativity, skill and sheer brilliance of our bakers has been a constant joy.

There's nowhere we'd rather be than eavesdropping in Cake Corner with Paul and Mary as they decide who should be Star Baker and who, sadly, will be leaving the tent. Or watching the action unfold against the clock, while our hopeful bakers slave over their biscuits, breads, pies and pastries. Of course Mel and Sue are always there to offer a shoulder to cry on, or to relieve the tension with a witty comment. Yes, fair enough – there have been occasions when one of the pair has leant on a muffin, broken a biscuit box, or eaten a vital ingredient, but let's not dwell on that.

This book celebrates all that we love about Bake *Off*. It's a chance to relive some of your favourite moments, get geeky as we delve in to some baking history, and catch up with some of your favourite bakers.

If, like us, you've always got room for more, arm yourself with a cup of tea and a generous slab of cake (nicely moist, not overbaked), and settle back for another slice of *Bake Off* action. Enjoy!

THE GREAT BRITISH BAKE OFF TEAM

BEFORE THEY WERE BAKERS

Can you identify these pint-sized bakers, who would eventually grow up to bring their baking brilliance to the tent in 2015?

GBBO BINGO!

Can you complete your *Great British Bake Off* bingo card? Every time you hear or see a classic *Bake Off* phrase or tradition, mark it off on your board. The first person to get a line (horizontal or vertical) wins!

Step One: Toss a coin to decide which bingo card you want.

Step Two: Settle down to an episode of *GBBO* with your bingo pen at the ready.

Step Three: Every time you hear or see an action marked on your card, cross it off.

Step Four: The first player to complete a horizontal or vertical line wins!

Suggested prize: A cup of tea and a biscuit

CARD 1

Bake Off BINGO!

1. PAUL DISAPPROVES OF A CHOICE OF INGREDIENT	2. A BAKER SITS CROSS-LEGGED WATCHING A CAKE RISE IN THE OVEN	3. MEL OR SUE PUT ON AN ACCENT	4. THE PHRASE 'BEAUTIFULLY MOIST' IS USED
5. A BAKER SUFFERS AN INJURY	6. ANY MENTION OF 'STIFFNESS'	7. SOMEBODY DROPS THEIR BAKE	8. MARY DESCRIBES SOMETHING AS 'SCRUMPTIOUS'
9. SOMEONE THROWS AWAY A BAD BAKE AND STARTS AGAIN	10. A SHOT OF A LAMB	11. THE PHRASE 'SOGGY BOTTOM' IS USED	12. MEL OR SUE ATTEMPT TO HELP A BAKER

CARD 2

Bake Off BINGO!

1. PAUL DESTROYS A CAREFULLY CONSTRUCTED BAKE WITH TOO MUCH PLEASURE WHILE JUDGING	2. MARY SHOOTS A DEATH STARE	3. A BAKER FORGETS TO USE A VITAL INGREDIENT	4. 'FROTHY PEAKS' GET A MENTION
5. MARY WEARS A JACKET OF MORE THAN THREE COLOURS	6. A BAKER CRIES	7. ANY PUN ON 'BUNS'	8. ANY FOOD IS SPAT OUT DURING JUDGING
9. THE PHRASE 'CREAMY FILLING' IS USED	10. MARY CONSUMES ALCOHOL WITH GLEE	11. A BAKE IS RAW IN THE MIDDLE	12. MEL OR SUE HUG A BAKER TO OFFER THEIR SUPPORT

AT HOME With ALVIN

What got you into baking?

When my daughter was seven years old, she came home from school and said we needed to bring cakes to the school fair tomorrow. My wife cooks, but she doesn't really bake. At that time I didn't cook or bake, so I got a cookbook from the shelf and made some cupcakes. They sold out and people were asking, 'Who made these!' My daughter was really proud. I made cupcakes for months. I've still got that original muffin tin and I want to pass it on to one of my children.

Tell us about your earliest food memory.

My seventh birthday, in the Philippines. My nan would always bake a Neapolitan cake and bring it to our house. I always looked forward to that.

What's your guilty food pleasure?

Sweets! Though I've recently enjoyed making entremets and mousse-based layered cakes. I'm working on a recipe for one now that has crème brûlée in the middle. I'll also be using a spray to glaze it, so it's quite complicated. After working four 12-hour shifts as a nurse, baking is something I look forward to enjoying at the weekend.

If you could invite anyone past or present around for tea, who would it be and what would you bake?

It's got to be Imelda Marcos! She just fascinates me; she's a larger-than-life personality. I met her once in the Philippines – I saw her eating in a patisserie and asked for her autograph.

If you could bake only one thing, what would it be?

Bread. It's one of those things that I'm really comfortable with and really happy making on a day-to-day basis. I once baked bread every day for three weeks until I felt I got it right. But secretly I don't want to get it right because I'm the sort of person that, once I've perfected something, I want to move on to something else. I don't want to find out I'm doing it right in case I get bored.

When you're not baking, how do you relax?

I like to walk, or sometimes I run. It used to be the thing I did before baking. I do run long distance.

Who do you like to bake for?

It's always got to be my family. I love it when they come down in the morning at the weekend and there's fresh bread. I don't mind getting up at 5.30am to second-prove it.

Which are your five favourite bakes?

Macarons, sans rivel (a Philippino dessert made from layers of buttercream, meringue and chopped cashew nuts), entremets or mousse-based cakes, various breads, balsamic onion batons.

What's your worst baking disaster?

Which one to choose? I've got loads. In 2011 I first tried to make choux pastry for a croquembouche. I was in the kitchen for nine hours, and at the end the whole thing collapsed. It was so frustrating – I wasted all the ingredients. Some of it was edible, but it wasn't a choux pastry croquembouche, so most went in the bin. My wife just shook her head.

What's the most surprising, unusual or interesting thing in your cupboard?

Pomegranate molasses, that's quite unusual. I haven't used it – in fact I can't remember what I bought it for!

What's your favourite kitchen gadget?

I've got this whisk and it's the first one we bought when we came to the UK. When I did *Bake Off*, I took it with me – it's a comfort thing. It's actually broken, the balloon end came undone, so I cut off the ends and now I use the remaining metals bits to flake caramel.

Describe your kitchen at home.

I have a small, basic kitchen. I'm happy with it but I wish I had a bigger one. When we moved to this house, some of my favourite baking trays didn't fit in the oven. When you're looking around a new house you don't take a baking tray with you to see if it fits in the oven, but next time I will!

What's your favourite ingredient to work with?

Vanilla. Whatever you do, if you add vanilla to anything, especially sweet things, it improves it.

Do you keep a recipe notebook?

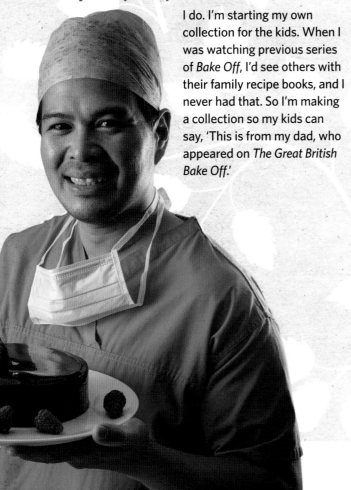

I do. I'm starting my own collection for the kids. When I was watching previous series of *Bake Off*, I'd see others with their family recipe books, and I never had that. So I'm making a collection so my kids can say, 'This is from my dad, who appeared on *The Great British Bake Off*.'

What did it feel like when you found out you'd been selected for *Bake Off* 2015?

I was at work when I found out, and it was the same feeling as when I saw my newly born children. I'm a big fan of the show: I've applied three times. It was like when you put a shell in your ear and you can't hear anything else! It was like that, amazing. My colleagues were so proud!

As a nurse, do you get given a lot of cake by grateful patients?

It's sweets mainly. But because we're in operating theatres, most of them are asleep, so they don't see us. It's the nurses on the wards who get the treats. They do bring us some, though.

Do you take bakes in to work to help everyone get through a night shift?

Yes I do, especially leaving dos or someone's birthday. People always say, 'Alvin, will you make the cake?' I do bring cake on a regular basis – it's so difficult to say no. I do enjoy it, though.

How did you prepare for *Bake Off*?

When I knew I was going to be on the show, I suddenly forgot how to make a Victoria sponge! Suddenly, I didn't know anything, so I needed to refresh my mind. The standard has got really high each year and it's moved on from basic stuff, so I did lots of reading and research.

What's your favourite *Bake Off* moment from a previous series?

My interest grew with Series Three. John Whaite's final bake, the chocolate glaze with the hair dryer. All my glazes are inspired by that recipe. I'm still trying to achieve that.

Who's your favourite past baker and why?

It's got to be John. I've got both his books. He's great.

DORRET

What got you into baking?

I learnt to bake at secondary school from the age of 11. Cooking was one of our compulsory lessons every week, which I really enjoyed. At school we made things that I never had at home, like scones. Mum never bought cakes from the shops, and there's a limited amount of sweet things in Jamaican culture.

Tell us about your earliest food memory.

I can remember mangoes. When my mum managed to get hold of some, we'd sit around her knees and she'd slice them for us. They were like treasures. It was hard getting mangoes in Preston in the 1960s.

What's your guilty food pleasure?

It's changed over the years because I find I have to be more careful with the calories now. I was totally into chocolate, but now I put my effort into really lovely patisserie. I would have two desserts instead of dinner if it weren't essential for the proteins and everything else!

If you could invite anyone past or present around for tea, who would it be and what would you bake?

One of the people I find fascinating is the Spanish film director Pedro Almodóvar. He lived through the Franco era and started off making these little quirky movies. He discovered Antonio Banderas, as well as Penélope Cruz. I don't know what I would make for him, though!

If you could bake only one thing, what would it be?

Probably Bakewell tart because I love it! It's got a nice shortcrust pastry, tasty jam, almond sponge and icing on top. It's a sweet hit with lots of textures.

When you're not baking, how do you relax?

I go to adult tap dancing classes. I also do salsa. My husband and I play squash, and it's war when we're on the court, which is better than whacking him with a frying pan! It can get quite intense, as we're both very competitive.

Who do you like to bake for?

Me! I like making things that I like. But I do like sharing too because when you get it right, people really enjoy what you've made. It's nice to be able to do that.

What are your five favourite bakes?

Bakewell tart, baked cheesecake, entremet cake, Christmas cake and Danish pastries.

What's your worst baking disaster?

Generally, I don't have to throw things in the bin. I did an entremet cake once and the mousse didn't set. It wasn't a disaster, though – it was still edible.

Tell us one thing about yourself that will surprise us.

My age! But I'm not going to tell you what it is!

What did it feel like when you found out you'd been selected for *Bake Off* 2015?

It was fantastic and scary at the same time. I didn't expect to be successful because I know how difficult it is and I've never really thought my baking was of a standard that would get me onto the show.

How did you prepare for *Bake Off*?

Last year my local supermarket ran a *Bake Off*-style competition on whatever the theme of the programme was that week, so I joined in and did very well. I got the equivalent of Star Baker. But all my life I've been preparing for *Bake Off*, really.

What's your favourite *Bake Off* moment from a previous series?

I liked the George versus the Dragon biscuit scene that Luis did. It was great, really clever, well thought out and well designed.

Who's your favourite past baker and why?

Can I have Dame Edna Everage in *The Great Comic Relief Bake Off*? When they criticised her bakes, she said, 'Well, Paul and Mary, they're not the only people in the world!'

What's the most surprising, unusual or interesting thing in your cupboard?

The most unusual thing at the moment is tonka beans.

What's your favourite kitchen gadget?

Probably my balloon whisk.It gives a lovely sheen, and all by your own efforts.

Describe your kitchen at home.

I've a small kitchen with quartz tops, which are brilliant for pastry and dough work. My husband does all the savoury cooking, while I just do the desserts and baking. I would like an induction hob because I hate cleaning hobs.

What's your favourite ingredient to work with?

I'm amazed at what you can do with an egg. It just blows my mind. I think it's fantastic watching them go from a sloppy see-through mess to fluffy, bright white things.

Do you keep a recipe notebook?

Yes. I don't go on the Internet – I'm proper old school. I write in all my cookery books too: what I've done, what I've changed, what I've discovered, or what I won't do next time.

YOUR BAKES FROM HOME

The first Signature Bake Challenge in 2011 was to create cupcakes. It's a bake that never goes out of style, and it allows the imagination to go wild. The bakers in the tent came up with great ideas, including Holly's Cherry Bakewell Cakes, and Mary-Anne's Banoffee creations. At home you've been just as creative, and here are some of your best efforts.

Cupcakes

1. Ice Cream Cone Cakes
Made by Julia from Boughton under Blean

A seaside-themed treat topped with icing 'ice cream' and a mini chocolate flake. When it comes to style, these cakes are hard to lick. We'll have 99, please.

2. Red Hot Velvet Cupcakes
Made by Louise from Sydney

If you like a bit of spice, these cupcakes are perfect for you. Sponge flavoured with paprika and cayenne, and topped with a fiery cinnamon icing, these fun cakes are crowned with a real dried chilli. Have a glass of milk to hand!

3. Gin and Tonic Cakes
Made by Carla from South Shields

These boozy beauties are best served chilled. G&T always comes served with a slice of lime, and these cakes do too!

4. Raspberry Mojito Cupcakes
Made by Kirsten from Troon

Another adults-only cupcake, this time inspired by the mojito cocktail. They would make the perfect birthday party treat.

5. Coffee Cups
Made by Jelena from Bexleyheath

This cupcake is a feat of engineering, with fully functioning cake cup handles. Make ours an extra large and frothy one, please!

6. Wimbledon Cakes
Made by Lesley from Greenock

We're not sure the pink frosting would pass the all-white rule, but we think the mini rackets on top are 'ace'. Game, set, and match, Lesley!

7. Flowerpot Cupcakes
Made by Helen from Glossop

If only we could grow cupcakes in the garden! These cakes are designed with horticultural panache and clever fondant icing work to create delicate, fun pots.

8. Baby Shower Cakes
Made by Sam from Ashford

A great idea to celebrate a baby on the way. The icing bonnets and dummies are cute as a button.

9. Christmas Tree Cakes
Made by Shanade from Brighton

The festive design on these cupcakes gets our baking bells jingling, and the combination of bright green icing and sugar sprinkle baubles makes for a seasonal showstopper.

10. Ghostly Hallowe'en Cupcakes
Made by Emily from Llanelli

Spooky and sweet, the perfect cupcake for a Hallowe'en party. The ghost sits on orange zest butter icing topping a chocolate sponge. Plenty of baking tricks, and what a treat!

11. Remembrance Sunday Cupcakes
Made by Rosemary from Fife

These were made for a charity bake off to raise funds for the poppy appeal. The poppy toppings are made from red fondant icing – a great idea.

HISTORY

Rise Up! A history of baking powder

If you think food intolerances are a modern issue, think again. The wife of Victorian chemist Alfred Bird couldn't eat anything containing eggs or yeast, so, in a demonstration of marital devotion, her husband dashed off to his lab and set about applying some science to the problem. In 1843, he came up with 'fermenting powder', later renamed baking powder.

Prior to the discovery, most bakes were raised with yeast, though during the fifteenth century, cooks in Italy had discovered that beaten egg whites incorporated into batter produced lighter, more aerated cakes. Sadly, the mechanical whisk wouldn't be invented for another 300 years, so the lowly kitchen servant had to beat the whites with a bunch of birch sticks, reeds or even feathers, often for hours.

By 1790, American Samuel Hopkins had developed 'pearl ash', made from the baked ashes of burnt wood. When this was mixed with acidic ingredients, such as sour milk, it caused an aerating action similar to that of baking powder. 'That's clever!' you might be thinking. Well, not exactly. Unfortunately, pearl ash also reacted with the fats found in most cakes to produce soap. As you can imagine, this made the cakes taste awful.

Some early Victorian recipes instructed the cook to add 'volatile salts', better known as smelling salts (ammonium carbonate). While this did raise the cakes, it made the kitchen reek of ammonia. After all this, baking powder must have seemed like a godsend.

Bird didn't really plan on revolutionising baking; he just wanted to make something his wife could eat. And being a classic British boffin, he initially didn't capitalise on this or other inventions. However, when dishes made with his creations went down well with friends at a dinner party, it led him to establish Alfred Bird & Sons in Birmingham in 1843.

Ironically, when he died in 1878, his obituary in the *Journal of the Chemical Society* mentioned at great length his work and research in the noble field of chemistry, while completely omitting his world-changing culinary efforts.

Is there a doctor in the kitchen?

Other brands of baking products from the dawn of cake chemistry include Dr Oetker, founded in Germany in 1891 by the eponymous Doctor August Oetker. Although a pharmacist by trade, his innovation was

actually in packaging baking powder into handy, ready-to-use portions, which he called 'backin'. When a portion was mixed with liquid and 500 g of flour, it guaranteed perfect baking results every time.

Cake-raising rivals

In the 1840s, Alfred Bird & Sons wasn't the only manufacturer of baking powder in Britain. George Borwick established his firm in Walthamstow, east London, in 1842, selling baking powder made to a recipe given to him by his father-in-law. Like Bird, he soon branched out into custard powder, and then powdered egg. His products won medals at trade shows, and his firm published many books instructing cooks how to use them.

Making cakes in ye olde days

- First buy your loose flour, dubiously fresh eggs, and rock hard sugar loaf from the grocer.
- Sift the flour to remove any insects or bits that might have fallen into the grocer's barrel.
- Using iron 'sugar cutters', snip off bits of sugar and grind them to a powder using a pestle and mortar.
- Separate the eggs and beat the whites with a bunch of birch sticks until soft peaks form (about two hours).
- Light the coal or wood-fired oven one hour before you want to cook.
- Fold the ingredients together and place in the hot oven.
- Hope for the best.

THE CUSTARD FACTORY

The original factory where Alfred Bird made his baking powder, egg-free custard powder and other foodstuffs is no longer there, but the building that replaced it is now an arts venue and community space called The Custard Factory.

BAKING AT THE SOUTH POLE

Bird's was one of many firms that supplied Robert Falcon Scott with products for his Antarctic expedition in 1901. Eight hundredweight (over 406 kg) of baking and custard powders were stowed on board RRS *Discovery* for its three-year mission.

Over the years the *Bake Off* tent has been the setting for more than its fair share of kitchen disasters. From dropped dishes to burnt buns, it's a pressure-cooker of potential nightmare scenarios. For the bakers, it isn't necessarily the blunders they make that matter, it's how they deal with the aftermath. Here's a handy guide to some tried and tested coping strategies for when the cake batter really hits the fan...

BAKING

DON'T PANIC!

WHEN IS A two-tiered cake not a two-tiered cake? When it has only one tier after being knocked onto the floor, of course. It was almost tears for tiers during Rob's first Showstopper, back in 2011, when his Chocolate Genoise took a tumble. So focused was he on smothering his chocolate creation in a delicious-looking ganache that he failed to notice every time he turned the cake-stand, he was moving it nearer to the edge. With inevitable results.

He may have uttered a few choice four-letter words (and we don't mean 'oops') that had to be bleeped out to spare Mary's blushes, but Rob quickly picked himself, and his cake, off the floor. With the help of Mel and Sue, and with Paul directing operations with military precision, Rob salvaged the only solid piece of cake that was left. Keeping his cool, he made the best of the dropped cake, basically by covering the misshapen lump in melted chocolate, and presenting it to Paul and Mary. True, it was a fraction of what they

were expecting (half to be precise), but what a fabulous fraction it was. The judges were duly impressed, with Paul saying that it tasted 'absolutely gorgeous', and Rob made it through to the next round.

WHAT WE LEARNT...

When disaster strikes, take a deep breath, see if there's anything that can be salvaged, and make the most of what you are left with. A dropped cake with a to-die-for taste is better than no cake at all.

CAKE DOWN!

$!£*!!!!

When two layers become one...

OK, keep calm, let's think...

Who needs two tiers anyway?

About that other tier...

BAD

DISTRACT FROM DISASTER

SO YOU'VE CURDLED your custard or your pie's gone pear-shaped – never fear, all is not lost. A little accessorising can work wonders, as demonstrated by Edd in 2010. This eventual winner wasn't always at the top of his game, and in Pudding Week his Rhubarb and Strawberry Suet Pudding Showstopper was a monumental flop, first refusing to come out of its bowl, and then collapsing onto the plate in a less than appetising manner. Mary had predicted the problem, saying, 'I'm really worried about those strawberries... You put them with sugar and they just go to a runny mess.' As ever, Mary wasn't wrong. Edd refused to be defeated by this

fruity mush, though. 'If you can't laugh about it, what can you do?' he said. Well, you can smother the whole mess in icing sugar, Edd. Which is precisely what he did.

How successful his secret weapon was is debatable. Paul described the finished bake as 'an absolute monstrosity of a car crash on a plate'. Not great then, but Edd survived and stayed in the tent. His pudding might have sunk, but his ship hadn't sailed...

WHAT WE LEARNT...

Icing sugar, like a layer of foundation after a heavy night out, can hide a multitude of sins. Apply liberally when needed.

Top of the flops.

Oh no!

Don't worry, I have a plan!

Icing sugar saves the day (sort of)!

BLAG IT!

WHAT'S THE BEST way to divert attention from your baking shame? Make it look like a deliberate act of artistry, that's how. The class of 2012's James showed some Caledonian craftiness when his Gingerbread Barn didn't shape up exactly as planned. Although meticulously designed on paper, when it came to being constructed, his biscuit building wasn't the barnstorming success James had hoped for. Time constraints meant he had to abandon plans for the barn to have all four walls – a minimum requirement for barns since time immemorial – leaving a more derelict-looking construction. But rather than admitting that his effort was structurally unsound, he draped it in sugar-spun spiders' webs and announced that he had always intended to create a bake that boasted some 'shabby shed chic'. Paul and Mary swallowed his story as enthusiastically as they did his tasty ginger offering, and James winged it all the way to the Final.

WHAT WE LEARNT...

That spin is as important in baking as it is in politics.

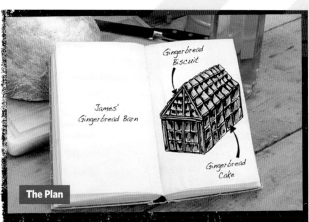

The Plan

The Reality

Of course this is how it's supposed to look!

I love your vision, James...

They fell for his whopper hook, line and sinker.

HOPE AGAINST HOPE!

WHEN THINGS GO very wrong, all you can really do is pray for a miracle. Say, for instance, you've added salt instead of sugar to your rum babas... We've all done it, haven't we? No? Just John, then, in 2012.

During the Technical Challenge in Cake Week, John's 1970s-style Rum Babas didn't exactly benefit when he confused salt and sugar (well, they do look quite similar). Once his error had dawned on him – and to be fair, it dawned on him very shortly after he tasted them – he swung into action with a troubleshooting strategy: (1) chop the salty tops off; (2) completely smother the rum babas in several tons of cream and fruit; (3) hope for the best.

Perhaps Paul and Mary would think his unconventional flavours were deliberate. After all, if salted caramel can become such a foodie phenomenon, why not salty sponge? The judges didn't quite see it like that, though, and Paul couldn't bring himself to swallow the botched baba. Luckily for John, he did enough with his Signature Toffee Apple Upside-Down Cake and a 'Hidden Hearts' Showstopper sponge to see him through, and eventually he went on to win the series.

WHAT WE LEARNT...

Even when you really foul up, all is not necessarily lost. As long as everything else you do is utterly brilliant.

They look delicious...

Let's just test a bit...

Yuk! Is that salt?

Will lashings of cream disguise the taste?

What the ?*@!*?

Ground. Swallow. Me. Up. Now.

It's been scientifically proven that eating cake improves your memory – just ask Mary and what's-his-name. How much of the activity in the tent have you managed to retain over the years? Test your knowledge against your family or friends in my giant *Bake Off* quiz.

THE GREAT BIG *BAKE OFF* QUIZ
ROUND ONE

▼ ▼ ▼ ▼ ▼ ▼ ▼ ▼ ▼ ▼ ▼ ▼ ▼

1. Who was the first-ever winner of *The Great British Bake Off* in 2010?

a. Ruth b. Jasminder
c. Edd d. Miranda

2. In 2014, Jordan produced a Japanese Kawaii Fraisier Swiss Roll. Apart from the crazy name, what was unusual about it?

a. It was flavoured with green tea.
b. It had decorative strawberries baked into the sponge.
c. It was bright pink.
d. It was shaped into a 'J'.

3. In 2011, which baker misspelt Sachertorte as 'Sachatorte' in the Technical Challenge?

a. Simon b. Holly
c. Mary-Anne d. Keith

4. What happened when 2014's Pastry Week Technical Challenge was revealed as a Kouign-amann?

a. None of the bakers finished in time.
b. Half the bakers used the wrong kind of pastry.
c. None of the bakers had heard of it before.
d. All the bakers burnt their creation.

5. From which country does Kouign-amann originate?

a. Belgium b. France
c. Germany d. Holland

6. Frances shaped her Chilli Chocolate and Ginger Breadsticks to resemble giant what in 2013's Bread Week?

a. Drumsticks
b. Toothbrushes
c. Matchsticks
d. Wooden spoons

7. In the 2010 Final, Ruth made cupcakes with an ingredient that Mary said she hadn't experienced in a cake before. What was it? (The answer is in this book.)

a. Turmeric
b. Fresh ginger
c. Wild garlic
d. Pink peppercorns

8. Class of 2012's John could not compete in the Pudding Week Showstopper because he had injured himself in the Technical Challenge. What had happened to him?

a. He fell off his stool during the judging and sprained his wrist.
b. He accidentally rubbed chilli powder in his eye.
c. He dropped a cake-stand on his foot.
d. He injured his finger on a food processor.

9. 'My wife said, "They won't like those biscuits!" She'll have to eat her words now.' Which class of 2014 baker said this about his Signature Farthing Biscuit bake?

a. Norman b. Luis
c. Richard d. Enwezor

10. A mix-up in the 2013 tent led to an ingredient in Howard's trifle going AWOL. What went missing?

a. His sponge fingers
b. His sherry
c. His caramelised apples
d. His custard

11. And which light-fingered baker accidentally pilfered the item?

a. Beca b. Kimberley
c. Toby d. Deborah

12. Complete the following quip, made by a jokingly competitive Holly during the 2011 Semi-final: 'We're all being terribly British and saying we just want everybody to do well. But inside we're saying _____?'

a. Your cake looks rubbish.
b. Die, one of you, die!
c. I loathe you with every breath in my body.
d. If I don't win this, I will never stop crying.

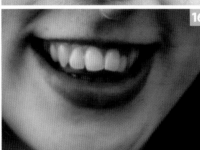

13. In 2014, which poet did Norman quote in his final week in the tent?

a. Robert Burns
b. William Wordsworth
c. Seamus Heaney
d. Pam Ayres

14–16. (near left) Can you identify these three bakers from their features?

a. James   b. Frances   c. Rob

17–21. (far left) Can you match the names to these tricky Technical bakes?

a. Schichttorte
b. Iced Fingers
c. Crème Caramel
d. Swedish Princess Cake
e. Charlotte Royal

22. In the 2012 Final, James suffered a crisis when making his United Chiffon Cake. What was it?

a. He burnt the cake.
b. He dropped it.
c. He used the wrong type of flour.
d. He forgot to add eggs to the mix.

23. Who was the last male baker to leave the tent in 2013? (The answer is somewhere in this book.)

a. Glenn   b. Howard
c. Robert   d. Ali

24. Which baker from 2014 is hidden behind this mammoth bowl of dough?

a. Martha   b. Kate
c. Diana   d. Claire

25. What TV show did Mary admit to getting hooked on during breaks between filming for *Bake Off*?

a. *Breaking Bad*
b. *Mad Men*
c. *The Only Way Is Essex*
d. *Geordie Shore*

The quiz continues on page 44
The answers are on page 124

SCONES, ETIQUETTE and afternoon tea

The Dutch East India Company introduced tea into mainland Europe around 1610, and by the 1650s it was on sale throughout London. The famous diarist Samuel Pepys wrote in September 1660: 'I did send for a cup of tee (a China drink) of which I never had drank before.' It's hard now to imagine a time when tea was so new and exciting that drinking it was worth noting in a diary.

A DECADE LATER, tea-drinking was firmly established, and it was women, barred from taverns and coffee houses, who now enjoyed it the most. Tea was a product to be prepared and enjoyed in the home, and, being an expensive commodity, would be kept locked securely in a wooden tea caddy in case of light-fingered servants.

The Chinese monopoly on tea was broken after plantations were established in Darjeeling and Assam in British-controlled India. This made tea much more affordable, and by the mid 1800s, afternoon tea had officially become a regular part of the day. With the arrival of gas lighting, the evening meal in fashionable houses was being taken later, so the afternoon selection of small sandwiches, cakes and biscuits taken around 4pm provided welcome sustenance and an excuse for another social gathering.

Lady Anna, Duchess of Bedford, held tea parties attended by the young Queen Victoria, where the gossip flowed like tea from the pot. As the author Henry Fielding once said, 'Love and scandal are the best sweeteners of tea.'

Of course, no afternoon tea these days would be complete without scones, but they didn't arrive on the tea table until the invention of baking powder in the 1840s. Their name brought with it a peculiarly English problem: does the pronunciation of 'scone' rhyme with 'John' or 'Joan'? According to a survey by University College London, 65 per cent of people opt for 'John', and just 35 per cent for 'Joan'. *The Oxford English Dictionary* notes that 'the first is associated with the north of England and the working class, while the second is associated with the south and the middle class'.

Once you've decided on the pronunciation, there's the small matter of how to eat them. Should you put the jam on first, or the cream? Cream on first is apparently the Devonshire way of doing it, while jam first is the Cornish way. Whatever you do, always use clotted cream, as whipped cream is considered frightfully vulgar.

Etiquette, gossip, scones and tea, what could be more British than that?

THE SCOTTISH SCONE

The word 'scone' – however you pronounce it – is actually Scottish in origin. It is thought to be derived from the Middle Dutch *schoon* (*broot*) meaning 'fine (bread)'.

Milk or tea in first?

Originally, most tea was taken black and the heat of it could cause the cup to crack, particularly if it was made of cheap china. Consequently, some ladies added the milk first to cool the tea. The more upper class the home, the more likely the milk was to go in last. The writer Evelyn Waugh once recorded a friend using the phrase 'rather milk-in-first' to refer to a lower-class person!

Broken cups and flying saucers

In the late eighteenth and early nineteenth centuries, China tea sets for large households often had 12 saucers but 24 cups – there were 12 large cups for breakfast, and 12 smaller cups for afternoon tea. The reason was that the cups often got broken first, resulting in orphaned and useless saucers. Of course, this enables present-day antique dealers to produce a 'full set' of 12 cups and saucers, but make sure you check that all the cups are the same size!

THUNDER AND LIGHTNING

If you fancy something different from the usual jam and clotted cream on your scone, try another Cornish version called 'thunder and lightning'. This sees the jam replaced with a drizzle of black treacle.

THE HEAVY TRADE IN POTTERY

Tea is relatively light in weight, so Victorian tea clippers – the ships that transported it from China to Britain – needed ballast for the return voyage. Their additional cargo of choice was Chinese pottery, and it is estimated that between 1684 and 1791, some 215 million cups, saucers, plates and pots were imported and sold in Britain.

EDD

The first ever batch of bakers to enter the *Bake Off* tent had no idea what to expect. Finding his job in banking less than exciting, Edd was ready for an adventure, and embarked on a journey of bread highs and pudding lows that would change his life forever. Looking back to 2010, Edd recalls the very first *Bake Off*.

2010

'A friend had seen an advert in the WI magazine for a TV baking show, and she immediately thought of me. I had already decided to try and make my hobby of baking into a career. I'd been turned down by a local catering college, and was attempting to teach myself in the evening after work. I didn't really think I'd actually make it onto the show, so to be there on the first day was exciting.'

CAKE WEEK

Hail Mary

'Everybody else turned up on day one with their beloved and battered Mary Berry books for her to sign. I remember feeling a bit sheepish that I didn't. I obviously knew who she was, but I'd never owned one of her books.'

The sponge that nearly wasn't...

Edd's first Signature Bake of a Caramel, Cinnamon and Banana Cake was well received by the judges, and he felt confident going into the Technical Challenge. But, as he recalls, it nearly went very wrong indeed...

'We had to make a Victoria sandwich. Paul and Mary came to talk to me literally minutes after I started baking. Mary asked if I was doing the classic method of beating butter and sugar together. A lightbulb went on in my head. Sugar! I went to grab the sugar, which I'd forgotten to put in. Thankfully, their little interruption reminded me not to miss out the vital ingredient. In the end I came first, but I very nearly came last!'

BISCUIT WEEK

Mmmmmacaron!

For his Showstopper, Edd created Rose and Raspberry Macarons that knocked the socks off the judges. Paul described them as 'excellent', while Mary's reaction was a low groan of pure pleasure that Edd will never forget.

'It was quite surreal. I was thrilled. I never thought one recipe would stay with me for so long. I still get emails asking if I am teaching macaron classes.'

BREAD WEEK

Self-discovery in dough

Going into Bread Week, Edd didn't feel overly confident. 'It wasn't something I made a lot of,' he says. But it turned out to be an undiscovered strength of his. Edd's Signature loaf was an Olive Oil, Fennel and Cumin Bread that Paul labelled 'technically excellent', and his Technical Challenge Cob Loaf was given top marks.

'For me, *Bake Off* was a process of learning about myself. I went into it very shy. The show kind of gave me a bit of a kick, a wake-up call to start believing I could do it.'

PUDDING WEEK

Edd's worst week

The bread high didn't last long, and Pudding Week saw Edd struggle. Rather than ending on a high, his Suet Pudding Showstopper completely flopped, failing to hold together when it came out of the mould.

'Not my greatest week, but I think everybody needs a dose of humility in their story!'

Although Mary and Paul agreed that he was in the danger zone, Edd survived and David left instead.

PASTRY WEEK

And relax!

'The Semi-final felt really relaxed. I honestly didn't feel that stressed. We filmed it in Cornwall by the sea; it was beautiful. We had a lot of fun that week.'

Mary liked his Chicken, Ham, Leek and Tarragon Pie, saying: 'You've got the seasoning right, it's good.'

FINAL

Firm friends

By now, the final three of Edd, Miranda and Ruth were very close.

'I was especially close to Ruth. She was so calm when she was baking. I think that because she had three young kids, she was used to multi-tasking. She always had a cup of tea on the go while she baked. We are still friends today.'

THE BIG FINISH

'That Final was huge! We had to bake for 35 people. I don't think any other series did as many different bakes in their Showstoppers as us lot.'

That didn't stop Edd excelling, and his Chocolate and Ginger Tart was particularly commended by Paul, who announced, 'That is lovely.'

WINNER!

When Edd was announced the very first *Bake Off* winner, it took a while to sink in.

'I was never a sporty kid, I had never won anything before. When they announced my name, it felt like a punch in the guts! I don't think it sank in properly for months, not until I saw it on TV.'

SINCE *BAKE OFF*...

One of the first things Edd did after winning was quit his job

'I worked for a bank where my job was basically to sue people. It was not a job I wanted to be in. Two days after winning, I handed in my notice. It felt like a very bold move. My plan was to try and get a job baking somewhere. It was a bit of a step into the unknown.'

Bake Off success changed everything for him

'I moved to London as the show started to air, and I remember being amazed by how many tweets I was getting. When I won I had lots of work offers. Raymond Blanc's team at Le Manoir offered me some work experience in their kitchens, which I took them up on. I never dreamed I'd end up doing TV work, or writing about baking for a living.'

He's published three books since winning *Bake Off*

'Of all the things I do for work, writing books is my absolute favourite. I am a naturally shy person and I don't like being the centre of attention. When I work on a book I'll spend at least six months in my kitchen on my own, just working on recipes, trying them out, tweaking them. I love that process.'

He's expanded into food styling

'I will work with a magazine to make dishes from a recipe and style it for the photographer to shoot. It's funny because I've done a lot of the *Bake Off* winners' recipes now. I've styled John's and Jo's recipes recently. I've also styled some of Luis' too. Thankfully, none of their recipes have been a nightmare yet!'

Bake Off has given him the life he wanted

'I always wanted a job that could make me happy and stress-free, and now I have that. I bake every single day. I can't think of a nicer thing to do for a living. I will always feel so grateful for how the show gave me the confidence to make changes to my life.'

THE GREAT BRITISH BAKE OFF
Hall Of Fame

We look back over six years of brilliant baking and celebrate some of the delights that have ended up on the judging table.

Kate's Red Velvet and White Chocolate Swiss Roll (2014)

PAUL: 'The swirl is probably one of the best we've got here.'

MARY: 'It's got wonderful decoration.'

Robert's Raspberry and Chocolate Cake (2013)

MARY: 'It's beautifully presented, lovely flavours, chocolate. You couldn't pass this without saying "Well done".'

Miranda's Three-tiered Chocolate Fudge Cake (2010)

MARY: 'It does look like a real celebration. Absolutely wonderful, simply delicious.'

PAUL: 'The outside chocolate is very bitter, the inside chocolate is very sweet, so you've got that nice blend between the two and it's still moist.'

When Paul asked the class of 2012 to make an eight-strand plaited loaf for their Bread Week Technical Challenge, it flummoxed the likes of Cathryn and Sarah-Jane. However, you have proved that plait-weaving isn't so difficult after all.

Plaited Loaves

1. Made by Ella from Newcastle

2. (a, b, c, d) Made by Kate from Birmingham

3. Made by Sabina from Leeds

4. (a, b, c) Made by Imogen from Orlando

5. Made by Lou from Solihull

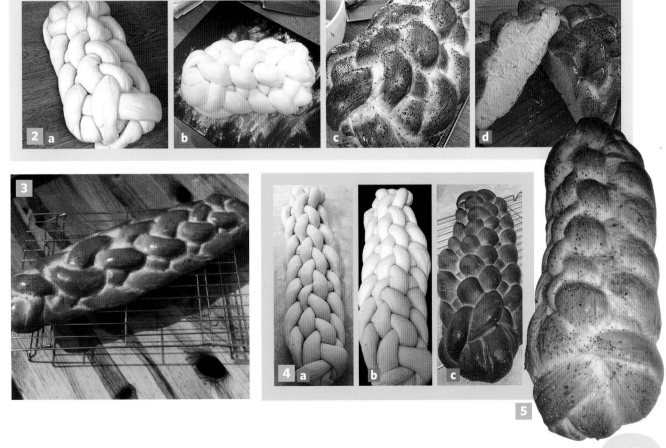

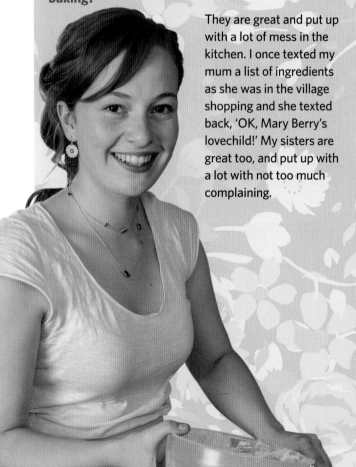

What got you into baking?

My family. We all bake, the men and the women, and everyone's a big foodie. I have loads of memories of Mum baking, or Granny doing stuff. There's no starting point as such, it's just always been there.

Tell us about your earliest food memory.

It's a Sunday morning and I'm in my pyjamas and we're making pancakes. We had this golden stand mixer from the 1960s. Mum would bake with it at night, and I would lie in bed upstairs and hear it whirring.

How supportive have your parents been of your baking?

They are great and put up with a lot of mess in the kitchen. I once texted my mum a list of ingredients as she was in the village shopping and she texted back, 'OK, Mary Berry's lovechild!' My sisters are great too, and put up with a lot with not too much complaining.

What's your guilty food pleasure?

Mascarpone eaten straight out of the tub.

If you could invite anyone past or present around for tea, who would it be and what would you bake?

Roald Dahl would be interesting. I would make him Eccles cakes – my dad's favourite – with a glass of whisky.

If you could bake only one thing, what would it be?

I'd make something that had a lot of processes and stages, like a huge wedding cake. It would be covered in macarons and icing, as well as fresh flowers and truffles, and it would be four tiers high. Hopefully, that would keep boredom at bay.

When you're not baking, how do you relax?

I love the cinema and I'll watch most stuff. I also do a lot of cooking, which isn't as stressful as baking!

Who do you like to bake for?

I'm quite happy to bake for anyone that's hungry, but I bake for my family more often than not.

What are your five favourite bakes?

White sourdough loaf, pistachio macaroon, chocolate chip cookies with muscovado sugar and sea salt flakes (it took me 50 different recipes to find one I was happy with), fennel ice cream sandwiches, and rhubarb and hibiscus spelt cake.

What's your worst baking disaster?

There have been many, but my mother is great at salvaging things from catastrophe. However, I did once forget the baking powder in a chocolate and buckwheat cake and it came out like a frisbee. That was the one thing my mother couldn't salvage!

What's the most surprising, unusual or interesting thing in your cupboard?

A mouse trap!

What did it feel like when you found out you'd been selected for *Bake Off* 2015?

I was sitting in my sister's bedroom. I'd had a rubbish day and was in a bad mood. I hadn't heard anything about *Bake Off* for ages. I thought, 'This is never going to happen. What am I going to do now? I suppose I'd better get a job.' Right then I got the call. I screamed at my mum. It was all very surreal.

How did you prepare for *Bake Off*?

I drew up a list of things I should practise, and I didn't rehearse a single one of them! There was so little time from being told 'You're on' to filming that preparation didn't really happen. You just had to go and do it.

What's your favourite *Bake Off* moment from a previous series?

Sue Perkins and James Morton downing whisky jelly shots. I thought that was quite entertaining when you consider it was probably filmed at 10 in the morning.

Who's your favourite past baker and why?

James Morton. I have both his books and they are instant classics. But I liked Chetna too. I wish I could do flavours like she can. She was the sort of baker you'd watch and think, 'I really want to eat that.'

What's your favourite kitchen gadget?

I'm pretty fond of spatulas. I also have a stand mixer, and the creaming attachment is the best.

Describe your kitchen at home.

We live in a converted barn, and the kitchen is the full height of the house. It's where we do most of our living, and it has a nice view looking over the glen. We have a blue Aga, and it was really hard getting used to a fan-assisted electric oven in the tent.

What's your favourite ingredient to work with?

Eggs. You can make meringues, custards, cakes, anything. Two of our chickens are called Mel and Sue, and they're very productive.

Do you keep a recipe notebook?

I've got 12 notebooks on the go at the moment, dotted all over the house. They're not particularly well indexed, however!

Tell us one thing about yourself that will surprise us.

I can do the splits, and my room is far messier than you would expect.

AT HOME
With
IAN

What got you into baking?

I've always loved cakes, so that's what started it. But when we moved to rural Cambridgeshire from Lewes in East Sussex, we missed the good cafés and bakeries. If I wanted good bread, I had to make it myself. I've always been quite practical. My wife works for an international aid organisation, and we were once in war-torn South Sudan. A turkey was being flown in to us for Christmas, but we didn't have an oven, so I built one. I also cooked a crumble for pudding. Not exactly the finest, but it was the only crumble for hundreds of miles around.

Tell us about your earliest food memory.

When I was younger my family lived in the States and I remember being tall enough to see over a shop counter. Much later, aged about 15, I remember eating a whole Battenberg cake and realising there was such a thing as too much sugar in one hit.

What's your guilty food pleasure?

Cheesecake for breakfast, but only when I'm hung over.

If you could invite anyone past or present around for tea, who would it be and what would you bake?

The Dalai Lama. I do photography for him when he comes to the UK. I'd make him a cake in the shape of the Potala Palace, as that was his old home in Tibet.

If you could bake only one thing, what would it be?

A good loaf of bread, the sort I make each week for the family. It's got black treacle and seeds in it. It's a good hearty, wholesome loaf.

When you're not baking, how do you relax?

I enjoy running, and doing up this ancient house of ours.

Who do you like to bake for?

For the family. That's my reason for doing it, to give them good food. I love to bake for big parties too.

What are your five favourite bakes?

My seeded loaf, any kind of fruity crumble, shortbread biscuits (one of the few things my son eats as he doesn't like much of my baking), scones and cheesecake.

What's your worst baking disaster?

I once tried to make a jam roly-poly. This grey blob came out of the paper I steamed it in. It didn't look good and it didn't taste good. We called it the coelacanth [an ugly-looking fish]. Also, I hadn't sealed up the greaseproof paper very well, and the suet covered everything. It was a nightmare to clean up. It put me off using beef suet for life.

What's your favourite ingredient to work with?

At the moment it's citrus oils, so there's lemon, lime and orange, but also bergamot. I'm using them in cakes and breads, but also in things like icing and chocolate.

Do you keep a recipe notebook?

I do now. I started one for doing *Bake Off*.

What's your party trick?

I can fire-breathe, how about that? I'm working on trying to do some cooking using this talent!

Tell us one thing about yourself that will surprise us.

In 1993 I climbed a 20,000-ft Himalayan peak.

Where's the most interesting place in the world you've photographed?

The photography I enjoyed most was a job I did for a safari company in Kenya. It was just wonderful. Meanwhile, the rest of the family were back here and struck down with the norovirus!

So do you combine photography and baking in some way?

I've been self-employed and worked hard all my life. That's one of the lessons I came away from *Bake Off* with: if you put your mind to something, you can achieve great things. All my working life has been about photography, that's plan A. Now this unusual plan B, baking, has come along and I'm not quite sure where to take it.

What did it feel like when you found out you'd been selected for *Bake Off* 2015?

Very surprising! I didn't consider myself one of the country's top amateur bakers, and I still don't, so it was a huge surprise. I still think, 'How did I get away with that?'

How did you prepare for *Bake Off*?

I gave up everything else and lived in the kitchen. I did lots and lots of practice and experiments. I learnt from my failures, and there were some expensive ones, baobab powder being one of them.

What's your favourite *Bake Off* moment from a previous series?

Probably Luis' Black Forest Cherry Tree from Series Five.

Who's your favourite past baker and why?

Probably Luis. I liked his design sense and neatness as it's something I can't do.

What's the most surprising, unusual or interesting thing in your cupboard?

It's got to be baobab fruit powder. It grows in Malawi and is a superfood. Of course this means that it's very good for you but tastes awful! I've tried to bake and cook with it and it still tastes terrible.

You're a big fan of using roadkill: tell us about that.

Yes, I've got a lot of roadkill in the freezer – things such as hare, deer and pheasant. I've saved so much money on meat in the past few years. I've made pies and put it in pasta dishes. I've even tried smoking it. Other odd food things I've done include making a giant Scotch egg from an ostrich egg.

What's your favourite kitchen gadget?

Probably my thermapen [digital food thermometer] – they're incredibly accurate.

Describe your kitchen at home.

It's a messy kitchen, a working kitchen, as I like to call it. It's pretty dated, horrible brown lino floor, and an Aga that I don't particularly like cooking on! But it is good for bread, that's all I use it for. I've also got a normal electric cooker.

YOUR BAKES FROM HOME

The class of 2012 gave us some brilliant designs cleverly concealed inside cakes for the Showstopper Challenge, ranging from John and his Hidden Heart Cake, to Stuart and Peter who both baked a Union flag into their sponges. A cake with a mystery centre is always fun. Here are some of your own creations.

Hidden Design Cakes

1. Berry Surprise!
Made by Debbie from Orkney

The exterior of this cake is exciting enough, but cut inside to reveal fresh strawberries and a stash of sweets! The sponge is vanilla-flavoured, coloured in pink and purple stripes to match the strawberries and blueberries on top.

2. Piñata Surprise
Made by Francesca from Wakefield

A thank-you cake with an extra special interior. Slice into it to reveal a hollow centre filled with surprise sweets, which then come cascading out.

3. Rainbow Piñata Cake
Made by Emily from Mold

Here's a brilliantly layered rainbow cake hiding a supply of sweets. It's a great celebration cake, perfect for a birthday.

4. Hidden Heart Loaf Cake
Made by Nikki from Salisbury

We can't hide our love for this tea loaf, which is masterfully baked to include a pink heart in every slice. Bake it for someone special.

5. Chap-tastic Choco Cake
Made by Shane from London

We're guessing Shane is a fan of chocolate! His creation – a chocolate sponge, topped with chocolate icing and chocolate sweets, all hiding even more chocolate sweets inside – is not for the faint-hearted!

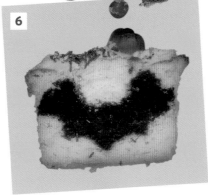

6. Bat Cake!
Made by Angela from Nottingham

The heart of this cake has a bat infestation, but it's not one we're in a hurry to get rid of. A smart idea for a Hallowe'en party, it has chocolate and vanilla sponges, creating a good contrast.

7. Boyfriend's Birthday Cake
Made by Emma from Amsterdam

As if the chocolate exterior of this birthday cake, made by Emma for her boyfriend's nineteenth birthday, wasn't fancy enough, the surprise centre is a kaleidoscopic marbled sponge.

8. Ice Cream Surprise
Made by Allison from Ayrshire

Ice cream and cake is the perfect combination, so we think this cone-shaped cake is great fun. Even better, once sliced into, the cake unleashes the perfect ice-cream topping – a handful of sweets!

9. Chequered Cake
Made by Kari from Isleworth

This colourful cake, made for a friend's daughter, must have taken Kari a long time to create. Neat blocks of brightly coloured sponge make for an unexpected centre to this birthday cake.

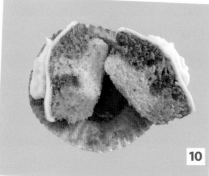

10. Rainbow Cakes
Made by Beth from Lesmahagow

Inside these cupcakes, Beth has created a fun swirl of colours by dividing up her basic mixture and colouring each part pink, green, blue or purple. The cakes would make for a great kids' party treat.

BUN, BAP, BARMCAKE, ROLL: what do you call a small round bread item?

You know, the sort you have on a side plate with a pat of butter, or sliced and stuffed with ham, cheese or even chips? A roll? A bap? A bun, barmcake or batch? Perhaps it's none of those, and instead you'd call it a cob, a stottie, or a muffin?

The answer will almost certainly depend on where you live, because these are just some of the regional names found around the United Kingdom for the humble bread roll.

According to research done by Dr Laurel MacKenzie and her linguistics students at Manchester University, the name 'roll' was most popular in the southeast and Scotland, while Wales and Northern Ireland favoured 'bap'. The northwest also went for 'bap', or else 'barm', while the northeast went mainly for 'bun' or 'stottie'. People in the Midlands, meanwhile, opted for 'cob', and occasionally 'batch'.

And that's just when it's plain old bread. When little extras such as dried fruits, lard or sugar start creeping in, the oven gloves really come off.

As recently as the 1940s, there were delightfully named regional bakes still being made in bakeries all over Britain. Anyone for tennis – and a Devonshire Chudleigh? Named after the West Country village of that name, these small bread rolls were enriched with butter and sugar, and best served with clotted cream and jam. If that sounds tempting, you might like to know that Cornish 'splits' are similar, but slightly bigger. These are often eaten hot with cream and jam, or treacle.

The intriguingly named Kentish 'huffkin' might sound like a slightly dim aristocrat from a Victorian novel, but it's actually another regional variation, also made from an enriched dough, though this time lard is used rather than butter. They each have a distinctive depression in the top, made by the baker's thumb prior to baking. Unsurprisingly, given their origin in the Garden of England, a traditional filling for them is pitted cherries.

The more unusual the ingredients, the more unusual the name seems to get. 'Hawkshead whigs', in which caraway seeds are added to a dough enriched with lard, are found in Cumbria. The name may be of Norse origin, perhaps baked as an offering to the god Wigga, but another suggestion is that the name comes from the Old German for 'wedge' or 'slice'. A wedge of whig certainly sounds more interesting than a bit of bread.

No prizes for guessing where Sussex Plum Heavies come from – but you might not guess what's in them. That's because they don't actually contain plums, but dried fruits as well as lard.

These wonderful regional goodies are becoming harder to find among the armies of baguettes, ciabattas and croissants found on every high street. Years ago, it seems, we just didn't know which side our bread roll was buttered.

MANX DUMB CAKE

One of Britain's most unusual regional bakes – dumb cake – is found on the Isle of Man. It was so called because it was eaten in silence on festival days throughout the year, such as saints' days, Midsummer's Eve, and particularly Hallowe'en and New Year's Eve. Young maidens would bake the cake from flour, water and salt in the ashes of the fire, and eat a piece while walking backwards to their beds. That night, according to folklore, they would dream of their future husband.

EDIBLE PLATES

In medieval times, hard flat discs of bread known as 'trenchers' were used as plates by the nobility. The juice from the food placed on them would soften them a little, after which they were given as alms to the poor. Some restaurants in North America continue this tradition with bread bowls – large rolls hollowed out and filled with thick soups such as New England clam chowder, or maybe stew or chilli. Certainly saves on the washing up!

SIZE MATTERS

Even the word 'bread' has changed meaning over the centuries. It was originally used to refer to any baked item, big or small, sweet or savoury. The word 'cake' came to be used for small bakes, while 'loaf' was used for large ones. The legacy of all this is still around today with words such as 'fishcakes', which are small, or 'meatloaf' which tends to be large.

Baking Breeds

The tent has always welcomed a wide variety of bakers, from old-school sticklers who prefer their recipes to be tried and trusted to spontaneous mavericks who throw not just caution but recipes, rules and weighing scales to the wind. There's no right or wrong way to approach *Bake Off*, as long as the finished result impresses Paul and Mary. Here we look at the five classic breeds of baker who wield their wooden spoons every year, and help you find out which type you are...

The Traditionalists

These bakers have crème anglaise running through their veins; their first word was probably 'genoise'. They learnt their craft from the generations who baked before them, and they have secret recipes that they will take to the grave.

NORMAN

Traditionalists have a tendency to stick to a well-trodden path, and can be too headstrong to deviate from what they know. Class of 2014's Norman comes from baking stock – his father and brother were both in the profession. Norman's simple style often paid off, with his classic Farthing Biscuits hailed as a triumph. However, traditionalists often find themselves out of their depth when they dare to stretch themselves, and are wary of anything new. Norman regarded pesto as 'exotic', and when he decided to 'jazz up' his meringue with lavender, it was a flavour fiasco. 'I've never had lavender in meringue and I don't think I ever want to again,' Mary declared, and Norman left the tent in Week Five.

CHRISTINE

A traditionalist will often be blessed with confidence in their abilities because they'll know their recipes inside out. When Christine took to the tent in 2013, she knew that her bakes worked – they'd been passed down from her mother and grandmother, and she'd tried them out on her husband and grandchildren. 'We're all trifled out at home,' she revealed during the Pudding Challenge, but it worked in her favour – she was Star Baker that week.

JO

While a traditionalist might be brimming with confidence, that doesn't mean they rest on their laurels. In 2011 traditional home cook Jo revealed that her family regularly grade her baking. 'Mine actually mark me out of ten,' she confided, before admitting they often award her just one point! Whether Jo then tells her family they can cook their own meals isn't known, but being used to tough criticism meant she was undaunted by Paul's often cutting verdicts and came out as the first female winner.

Most likely to say: 'This was my gran's favourite recipe…'

Least likely to say: 'Today I'm experimenting with caramelised kale and bergamot extract…'

THE SCIENTISTS

More comfortable in a white coat than an apron, the scientific baker knows that the secret to a good bake is in the chemical structure of the ingredients. It's not just a case of mixing flour, sugar and water, but of combining elements from the Periodic Table, often at a subatomic level (no, we haven't a clue what this means either).

James

From 2012's baking bunch, James – with his medical background and an approach to kitchen craft that combined care and chemistry – is the archetypal scientific baker. In Bread Week he proved just how serious he was when he produced a sourdough yeast he'd been cultivating as a hobby for eight years.

Jordan

There's definitely something about scientific bakers and yeast. Just two years after encountering James's carefully cultivated leavening mixture, we were introduced to Jordan's 'pet yeast' named Yorick.

Rob

In 2013, Rob – a space satellite designer – controlled his creations with a laboratory-like approach. 'It's all about crystal structure,' he declared while melting sugar. But science isn't the answer to everything. While he slaved over a sugar-mix 'edible glue' to cement together his biscuit tower in the shape of a Dalek (what else?), Rob failed to compute that the biscuits needed to impress the judges on more than just their looks. For Rob it was 'Exterminate!' from Paul and Mary, whose formula for winning will always be: 'Make it taste good.'

Most likely to say: 'The Maillard reaction is a form of non-enzymatic browning caused by heating amino acids and proteins.'

Least likely to say: 'Oooh, the dough's doubled in size. I wonder why that is.'

A pie isn't just pastry and filling – it's an edible work of art. That's the philosophy of the designer-baker, whose creativity with colours, shapes and textures – if not always with flavours – is their trump card. They will craft an aesthetically pleasing or daringly avant-garde bake that visually at least will far outshine any run-of-the-mill efforts. The designer-baker uses moodboards, sketches, templates, computer modelling and every shade of food colouring known to man. They see the cake stand as a blank canvas on which to unleash their inner Picasso.

the designers

Frances

Crowned queen of design in 2013, Frances took baking artistry to a new level. She transformed the humble breadstick into a spectacular matchstick-inspired installation piece, and created a jenga game out of her Banoffee Traybake. She might have occasionally been accused by the judges of putting style before substance, but there was no denying that her dishes were visually stunning, and her originality helped her to win the competition. Loaf of bread masquerading as a giant cappuccino, anyone?

Miranda

The class of 2010 stood back in awe at Miranda's presentation prowess. A tent trail-blazer for giving dishes that extravagant finish, her very first Showstopper was a beautiful triple-tiered chocolate bake adorned with homemade edible buttons bursting out on wires. So it was rather surprising to see Miranda's chances of winning slip away in the Final when she produced cupcakes that Paul deemed 'childlike'. If Paul and Mary think the design has become more important than the taste, they will be ruthless. Bakers beware!

Luis

Another dazzler with his designs in 2014 was Luis. His Dobos Torte was topped with a three-dimensional caramel recreation of his wife's favourite landmark, The Cage in Lyme Park, Cheshire. In a rare *Bake Off* moment, Paul even apologised for destroying the monumental work of art with his judging knife.

> **Most likely to say:** 'No need to taste it, Mary, just admire its beauty...'
>
> **Least likely to say:** 'I don't like fussy finishing touches.'

The Free Spirits

Those in this category are the instinctive bakers with an innate ability to combine ingredients and flavours. They're not afraid to deviate from a recipe – if they use a recipe at all. Their wild-child approach to baking can appear completely chaotic, but they are often able to wing it, pulling out bakes that will knock your socks off. Forget neatly levelled-off measuring spoons and carefully monitored oven temperatures, these rock 'n' roll bakers are out to smash the system and whip things up in their own special way.

I'd better just try and blag this bake...

Kate

Tousle-haired rebel Kate, resident of 2014's tent, baked to the beat of her own drum. When every other baker had their Kouign-amann dough in the proving oven, she had hers in the fridge. In Pies and Tarts Week, while working her hot-water-crust pastry for her Showstopper Rhubarb, Prune and Apple Pork Pies, she announced, 'I'm going to just dive in with my hands.' While everybody fussed with spirit levels and pre-cooked fillings, Kate got creative with her flavours and was awarded Star Baker.

Ruby

The class of 2013's quietly instinctive baker, Ruby subtly cast aside preparation on many an occasion and admitted in nearly every episode that she was going to try and wing it. 'It didn't work at all at home, so it's an improvement on that,' she said about her Tea Loaf; and 'We'll just see what happens,' as she chucked a foil 'hat' on her Apricot Couronne to stop it browning. During Bread Week she revealed the secret to her baking style: 'When I'm at home, I'm watching TV whilst I'm baking, and I take a break every now and again, and then I get distracted. I never bake with this concentration or speed ever.' Her laid-back student attitude saw her named Star Baker that week, and she catapulted into the Final, to nobody's surprise apart from her own!

Jasminder

The *Bake Off*'s original wild card was 2010's Jasminder. Fearlessly, she added popping candy to meringues, and chucked a Mars bar into her Pain au Chocolat. In fact, it was only when she toned down her flair for the unpredictable in the Semi-final, producing a 'bland' (her word!) traditional Chicken and Mushroom Pie, that she didn't impress Paul and Mary and left the tent. Chicken and popping candy pie next time?

Most likely to say (if a bake goes well): 'Of course I knew it would turn out like that.'

Least likely to say (if it doesn't): 'Of course I knew it would turn out like that.'

The Perfectionists

Neat, tidy and ever so slightly obsessive about measurements, the meticulous baker wouldn't dream of serving up a plate of biscuits if they weren't all the exact same size, colour and texture. They won't go near a recipe without a plan of action and a ruler stuffed in their back pocket. They'll weigh their flour three times, and then once more just to be on the safe side, and if their bake fails to rise, it'll send them spiralling into a world of doom.

Holly

Back in 2011, Holly got a reputation for being a perfectionist during her time in the tent. 'I get quite upset if things don't go well,' she admitted. Holly weighed her Stilton and Walnut Buns on miniature scales for precision, and sized up her Strawberry and Custard Melts with her trusty ruler. Her neat and tidy approach was well received by the judges, and she rocketed to the Final, where she was pipped to the post by Jo.

Most likely to say: 'One of my custard tarts is a millimetre smaller than the others. I'll have to start again.'

Least likely to say: 'The scales are broken? No problem – I'll just take a wild guess...'

Brendan

Another baker who ran a tight and tidy ship was Brendan. Approaching his Petits Fours for the 2012 Semi-final, he said he was striving for 'Absolute uniformity. That might sound like I have perfectionist tendencies, and I do. It can make me very difficult to live with.' (If we could eat Brendan's Lime Curd Choux Cygnets on a daily basis, we would try to put up with it!)

Richard

Class of 2014's Richard never went near his oven without a pencil behind his ear. A builder by trade, it was his ethos of putting down strong, well-planned foundations for his bakes that got him to the Final.

WHAT KIND OF BAKER ARE YOU?

Take this quiz to find out what your baking style says about you.

1. You feel like baking a cake – what would you do first?

a. Dust off your grandma's recipe notebook, except it hasn't got any dust on it because you use it every day.
b. Find every single utensil you'll be needing, and line them up perfectly on your thoroughly scrubbed work surface.
c. Draw a detailed picture of how you want the bake to look.
d. Decide to invent a new cake, using whatever ingredients take your fancy.
e. Measure every ingredient twice before combining anything.

2. What's your most important baking aid?

a. A wooden spoon
b. An industrial-standard thermometer
c. A selection of 60 different food colourings
d. A cup of tea
e. A measuring tape

3. What's your favourite bake to create in the kitchen?

a. Toad-in-the-hole followed by trifle
b. Sourdough bread, using a starter yeast you've kept in the airing cupboard for the past five days
c. A birthday cake in the shape of Ben Nevis for a friend who's a keen walker
d. You don't have a favourite – it changes every day
e. Anything miniature, ornate and quite fiddly

4. How best would you describe your kitchen at home?

a. A kitchen, of course, what else?
b. A laboratory
c. An artist's studio
d. A play area
e. Extremely tidy

5. Your bake goes disastrously wrong: how do you react?

a. You laugh, but make the decision never to try anything as new-fangled as that again.
b. You carry out an in-depth, evidence-based investigation of what went wrong and why.
c. You hide it all under an awe-inspiring decorative finish made from Italian meringue.
d. You shrug your shoulders and say, 'C'est la vie.'
e. You wouldn't know, as this has never happened.

6. The most important thing in baking is...?

a. Great taste
b. Consistency
c. Appearance
d. Improvisation
e. Preparation

9. What do you listen to while you bake?

a. *The Archers Omnibus*
b. Kraftwerk
c. Jazz
d. Your iPod on shuffle play
e. Mozart

7. Which of the following is your idol?

a. Your mother
b. Albert Einstein
c. Vincent van Gogh
d. The Buddha
e. Steve Jobs

10. How do you do your food shopping?

a. You visit your local butcher, baker and grocer, avoiding the supermarket.
b. Your smart fridge orders online for you.
c. You buy the products with the best packaging.
d. You pop into the shops as and when you need something.
e. You do a weekly shop, with every day's meals pre-planned.

8. Which of these recipe books would you be tempted to read if they were real?

a. *The A-Z of Family Cooking: Recipes from My Mother*
b. *Baking That Goes with a Bang – Literally*
c. *It's a Piece of Cake! 1001 Amazing Designs Made from Sponge*
d. *Amaranth to Zuccotto: Baking That Goes with the Flow*
e. *Perfect Puddings Every Single Time without Exception*

ANSWERS

If your answers were mostly: a. – you are a Traditionalist: Granny would be proud; **b.** – you are a Scientist: you're a baking boffin; **c.** – you are a Designer: it's all about the look; **d.** – you are a Free Spirit: you dance to your own beat; **e.** – you are a Perfectionist: nothing you do is ever half-baked.

Time to get your brain in gear for the second part of our baa-baa-bumper quiz.

THE GREAT BIG *BAKE OFF* QUIZ
ROUND TWO

▼▼▼▼▼▼▼▼▼▼▼▼▼

1. At 17 years old, who was the youngest baker to appear on *The Great British Bake Off*?

2. And who, at 69, was the oldest?

3. Yasmin suffered a setback while baking her Croquembouche in 2011. What was it?

a. She dropped her choux buns on the floor.
b. She couldn't get the cone structure to stand up.
c. She put too much rosewater in the mixture.
d. She burnt her fingers in the hot caramel.

4. In 2014, Mary and Paul could not agree which baker should leave the tent in European Cake Week. How did they resolve the conundrum?

a. Two bakers left.
b. They asked Mel and Sue to make the final decision.
c. No bakers left.
d. They arm-wrestled to decide it.

5. In 2011, what did Simon use this contraption for in his first challenge?

a. To hang spun sugar from.
b. To loop his breadsticks around.
c. To display his cupcakes.
d. To bash his head with when the pressure got too much.

6. In 2014 Nancy 'forgot' Paul's name. What did she call him instead?

a. Ol' blue eyes
b. The male judge
c. The Scouser
d. Judge Dread

7. What mode of transport did James construct out of Paris-Brest choux for one of his Showstoppers in 2012?

a. A motorbike
b. A canal boat
c. A bicycle
d. A Routemaster bus

8. What was unusual about Luis' doughnuts in 2014?

a. They were flourless.
b. They were savoury.
c. They were inspired by cocktails.
d. The dough was multicoloured.

5

9. In Dessert Week in 2013 Frances took inspiration for her Petits Fours from which famous ballet?

a. *Swan Lake*
b. *The Nutcracker*
c. *Sleeping Beauty*
d. *Coppélia*

10. And how did Frances display them?

a. On a pile of sheet music
b. On a record
c. In a box of ballet shoes
d. On a miniature stage

11–15. (opposite) Can you name these tricky Technical bakes from previous series?
a. Battenberg b. Classic French Tuiles c. Lemon Soufflé d. Queen of Puddings e. Fraisier Cake

16

16. Which baker leaving the tent in 2013 is the filling of this 'Mel and Sue sandwich'?

a. Deborah b. Lucy
c. Christine d. Beca

19. What kind of Showstopper did Ryan make in 2012's Pie Week, which Paul described as 'sheer perfection' and earned him Star Baker?

a. Blueberry pie
b. Pumpkin pie
c. Lime and ginger pie
d. Peanut butter pie

20. When Mary Berry appeared on *Bake Off*'s sister show, *An Extra Slice*, she revealed, 'If I was doing something with ____, would I make it? No, I wouldn't – it comes in nice packets!'

a. Fondant icing b. Custard
c. Sponge fingers d. Filo pastry

17. In 2013, Glenn modelled his Shortbread and Macaroon creation on which fairground attraction?

a. A fun house
b. A coconut shy
c. Dodgems
d. A helter-skelter

18. What unusual object did Norman use to sift icing sugar in 2014?

a. A shower cap with holes in it
b. A golf ball wrapped in a muslin cloth
c. A plastic carrier bag
d. The rose of a watering can

21–25. Can you match the names to the bakers below?
a. Urvashi b. Ali c. Enwezor
d. Natasha e. Ben

The quiz continues on page 92
The answers are on page 124

45

EDIBLE MYTHS: why some foods aren't what they seem

That pub favourite, the ploughman's lunch, conjures up images of a ruddy-cheeked nineteenth-century farmhand enjoying beer, cheese and a chunk of freshly baked bread before picking up his scythe to gather in the harvest. It's such a pleasant image that you can't help falling for it. Trouble is, it's a complete and utter fib.

The ploughman's lunch, as we know it today, was invented for a marketing campaign devised by the English Country Cheese Council (ECCC) in the late 1950s. They wanted the public to eat more cheese, and thought the pub was the place to do it. Cheese could easily be kept cool in the cellar with the beer, and all that remained was to get the daily bread from the local village baker.

The genius of the ECCC's plan was that every part of Britain could use its own regional cheese: Cheddar in the West Country; Red Leicester or Stilton in the Midlands; and Lancashire, Cheshire or Wensleydale in the north. The idea was designed to sell a romantic notion of England's pastoral past, right at the time most ploughmen were becoming obsolete.

Other foods that aren't as old as some people think include the Italian bread ciabatta. You might imagine it's been around since Roman times, but it was actually invented in 1982. A patriotic baker called Arnaldo Cavallari, from Adria, near Venice, was concerned at the rising dominance of French baguettes, so he developed a home-grown alternative that could be filled in just the same way.

Myths and mystery also abound in how some other bakes were invented, and many bakes and puddings are attributed to 'lucky accidents' in the kitchen. Take tarte Tatin, said to have been 'created' by hotelier sisters Stéphanie and Caroline Tatin in the town of Lamotte-Beuvron in the early twentieth century, when one of them 'accidentally' left some apples cooking too long and covered the results with some pastry. In fact, such upside-down apple bakes were popular in the Sologne region of France long before the sisters opened their hotel there. It's fair to say, though, that they helped to establish its popularity.

A similar English story is the 'accidental' creation of Bakewell pudding, supposedly in the 1860s. It too has familiar roots – a hotel, a distracted cook in the kitchen, a mistake in the baking, and diners who love the result. But, sadly, this is unlikely to be true, as the pudding was around long before that date.

When it comes to baking, then, things aren't always what they seem.

So what did ploughmen eat?

Most agricultural workers took their meals at home at the end of the day. If they did take any food into the field, it would have been a cold lump of cooked oats and grains with maybe a few nuts or whatever they had to hand. This, when you think about it, is very similar to a modern-day office worker snacking on a cereal bar.

Fortune cookies

If you think that fortune cookies are an age-old snack from China, you'd be mistaken. These crunchy biscuits, complete with a little message inside, were actually invented in Japan in the nineteenth century. Japanese restaurants on the West Coast of America also offered them, but many of the restaurateurs were interned when World War II started. Chinese restaurants decided to fill the gap, and as Chinese food became popular in 1950s America, the fortunes of the fortune cookie grew too. Interestingly, they're completely unknown in China.

Lea & Perrins Worcestershire sauce

The chance creation of this iconic condiment has more than a whiff of Victorian PR spin about it. The story goes that around 1830, a local nobleman, Lord Arthur Sandys (1792–1860) returned from India and asked two local chemists, John Wheeley Lea and William Perrins, to make him a spicy sauce similar to one he'd enjoyed on the subcontinent. They gamely gave it a go, but the end product tasted absolutely disgusting. Rather than throwing it away, they 'conveniently' left it in their cellar. A few years later – ta-dah! – they found that the vile brew had mellowed into a fine, tangy, slightly sharp sauce. It does beg the question what on earth made them taste it, but however it was created, cooks have been adding a glug or two to savoury pies and puddings ever since.

YOU WILL LIVE A LONG LIFE

Hall Of Fame

Brendan's 'All American' Chiffon Pie (2012)

PAUL: 'It's quite an elegant-looking pie. It's well baked. Sharp, sweet, flavours coming through. Well thought out. Great base.'

MARY: 'Really well baked.'

Frances' Rainbow Picnic Pie (2013)

PAUL: 'It's impressive. I like the lattice-work on top. Very, very neat layers.'

MARY: 'It's a very good bake underneath and you've got crisp, sharp corners. The individual flavours taste very good. You've cleverly seasoned it.'

Ryan's Lime and Ginger Pie (2012)

MARY: 'I think it looks absolutely lovely, so fresh. Sheer perfection.'

PAUL: 'You've absolutely nailed that. The flavour of that lime coming through, that is very special. That's a very nice pie, that's fantastic.'

Luis' Tropical Manchester Tart (2014)

MARY: 'The custard has got a lovely shine.'

PAUL: 'Nice and thin pastry, sides and bottom. You've got the sharpness of all the citrus fruits coming through really well. Very difficult to critique.'

Ruby's Plum Jam Roly Poly (2013)

MARY: 'It absolutely is beautifully flavoured. It's lovely.'

PAUL: 'I love the plums going through it. If that was on a menu, I would choose that.'

Ruth's Red Pepper Mini Tart (2010)

MARY: 'The pastry is beautifully brown.'

PAUL: 'Very thin and it tastes fantastic.'

YOUR BAKES FROM HOME

In 2013 Beca made a Semi-final Showstopper that defied the normal conventions of cake. Her Butternut and Pecan 'Cheesecake' resembled a great wedge of Cheddar, complete with mice feasting on it. You have been just as creative when it comes to cakes that are cleverly disguised. These are some of our favourites. Consider our minds boggled!

'You Won't Believe It' Cakes

1. Noodle cake
Made by Linh from Nottingham

Linh says this birthday cake was inspired by her family's culture and love of Chinese food. Our favourite parts are the life-like boiled egg and the trailing noodles over the side of the bowl.

2. Cheeseburger
Made by Lauren from Banbury

We'd get seriously confused biting into this cake, which looks so much like a burger that we'd be tempted to smother it in ketchup. Lauren says she created the perfect dome shape for the 'bun' by baking sponge in a pudding bowl.

3. Sushi
Made by Paul from Banbury

Evoking traditional Japanese food in cake form takes some hard work, but we think Paul's played an absolute blinder. The rice effect in the sushi is created with coconut shavings.

4. More sushi
Made by Holly from Swansea

This Sushi cake is also fantastic. We especially love the little wasabi and pickled ginger accompaniments. Just make sure you don't dunk this in soy sauce.

5. Pizza
Made by Robin from London

A slice of pizza is almost as tasty as a slice of cake, so we think this bake is a great combination of both. Robin created the baked crust effect by taking a blowtorch to the icing!

52

6. Sunday lunch
Made by Jo from Wolverhampton

This is a lemon Madeira cake masquerading as a plate of roast pork with all the trimmings! All the meat and veg are created using coloured marzipan, while the pieces of 'crackling' are actually wine gum sweets coated in sugar.

8. Steak and chips
Made by Victoria from Steeple

A fan of steak and chips would have a hard time resisting this chunky cake, fashioned as a slab of prime beef. The 'searing' on the surface adds a realistic touch, and the peas and chips work really well alongside. A rare cake, very well done.

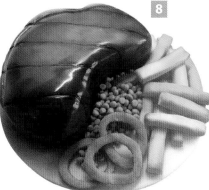

9. Cheeseboard
Made by Emma from Walton-on-Thames

A whole new kind of cheesecake! Made for Emma's 'foodie' better half, this cheeseboard is such a fun idea. The splash of red wine made from icing is the finishing touch to a fine design.

10. Fish fingers and custard
Made by Tat from Shrewsbury

Inspired by an episode of *Doctor Who*, where the Doctor reveals his favourite snack is fish fingers in custard, this wacky cake was made for a children's party. The bowl of custard is marzipan-covered almond cake, and the coating on the fish finger cakes is created with whizzed-up cake crumbs!

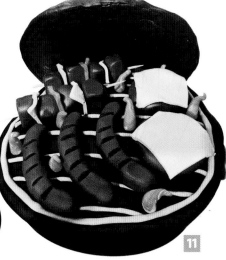

11. Barbecue
Made by Jo from Bristol

Is it a cake or is it a barbecue? A brilliant idea from Jo combines the two, complete with melting cheese and sizzling kebabs. Throw another sugary shrimp on the barbie!

7. Wine bottle
Made by Cathy from Kent

Totally alcohol-free, but just as satisfying. The bottle is made from chocolate cake and rests on a nest of 'straw' made from white chocolate shavings. We'll toast to that!

AT HOME *With* MARIE

What got you into baking?

In 1983 we moved to Paris for around five years, and there were all these impressive bakery shops. We had nothing like that in Scotland. I had time on my hands while the children were at school and my husband was at work, so I learnt to bake. I became inspired by what was normal in France.

Tell us about your earliest food memory.

My mother was one of ten, and all the family lived close by. I used to visit one aunt and she made this incredible chicken broth, so I really looked forward to that. I also remember going to another aunt's house and her saying, 'Would you like some black pudding in the morning?' and thinking I was going to get custard for breakfast!

What's your guilty food pleasure?

I'm not that keen on chocolate, but I do like most sweet things. We have a thing here in Scotland called tablet [a kind of hard fudge]. I have to limit myself on that. I've tried it everywhere I've been because it's all over Scotland.

If you could invite anyone past or present around for tea, who would it be and what would you bake?

It would have to be Sean Connery. I knew him in Glasgow in the 1960s. I'd bake him a steak pie because I know he likes it, and I'd like to see Sean again.

If you could bake only one thing, what would it be?

Shortbread. It's easy to make and you can eat it any time.

When you're not baking, how do you relax?

I read a lot, I play golf and do zumba classes, and I love looking after my grandchildren. We have a Monopoly board set up on the table, and every time they visit we continue the game. I cheat, though, and add more money to their wee piles so they can keep playing. They're such characters. I was making toffee the other day and there was a wooden spoon sticking out of the pan and one said, 'Why's there a breadstick in it?'

Who do you like to bake for?

Family and friends. If I go to friends for dinner or even for coffee, they expect me to bring a cake of some sort.

What are your five favourite bakes?

Pear and frangipane tart, walnut and coffee cake, meringues, curry with homemade naan breads, and any pastry with ingredients like roasted vegetables or goats' cheese.

What's your worst baking disaster?

It's a learning process with me. The first time I tried to make bread in Paris, it was just awful. I think the bin broke when I put it in. And it took so long to make, that was the most annoying thing! I've not had too many disasters recently because I stick to things I know I can do.

What's the most surprising, unusual or interesting thing in your cupboard?

Probably cubeb peppers [dark dried peppers native to Java]. They were for a loaf I was making, but I tried one and it was revolting, so they're still sitting there. What else have I got in here? I've got a lot of gold and silver in my cupboards, as well as pearl sugar and coloured wonton wrappers!

What's your favourite kitchen gadget?

A hand whisk, would you believe? It's one of those things I just feel comfortable with. I got it when we were in France and it's lasted all this time. It's a metal one and something that I treasure.

Describe your kitchen at home.

It's quite big and the nicest thing is the view, which is spectacular. I look onto the mountains. I have a large wooden kitchen table in it and I also have a wine bottle cooler. I've got lots of workspace. It's clean and tidy. I even keep my toaster in a cupboard because I don't like it out all the time.

What's your favourite ingredient to work with?

I do actually like working with chocolate, though I don't like eating it too much. With chocolate you can do so many different things. I love making big chocolate cakes, and things like Black Forest gateau.

Do you keep a recipe notebook?

Yes, several. I've started making one for my daughter, which I've been promising her for about ten years now. Some of the recipes in it came from my mother and my aunts. I know there's lots of recipe books out there, but it's nice to have a personal one, isn't it?

What's your party trick?

I have a guitar and I sing 'These Are a Few of My Favourite Things' from *The Sound of Music*. We all grew up singing in choirs. We're a very musical family. In Scotland we all do a turn.

Tell us one thing about yourself that will surprise us.

I was a disc jockey in Glasgow in the 1960s.

What did it feel like when you found out you'd been selected for *Bake Off* 2015?

I couldn't believe it. My daughter had put me in for it and I didn't know anything about it. In fact, when the call came I thought it was my son kidding me. It was a bit of a shock and I never thought for a minute I'd get through to the last twelve. I was in shock for about three weeks, then I started panicking!

How did you prepare for *Bake Off*?

I immediately started making bread because that was my weakness. I knew my cakes were fine, pastry wasn't too bad, but I needed to work on bread. Every day I was up at 6am and baking till midnight. Do you know, my oven light blew out twice, that's how much it was on.

What's your favourite *Bake Off* moment from a previous series?

I like it when they do Showstoppers. Like when they were making Fondant Fancies, and they were all awful, but they still soldiered on. I thought that was lovely. Mary made it look so easy, but I know how difficult they are.

Who's your favourite past baker and why?

Since I'm into bread, it's got to be James Morton. He's not only good-looking, he's a very creative young man.

AT HOME
With
MAT

What got you into baking?

When I started at the Fire Brigade, the shift pattern meant four days on, four days off, and I needed something to do on my off days. The first thing I made was a packet of bread mix. I really just added water, but it got me started. I've been baking for two years now. It's something productive to do.

Tell us about your earliest food memory.

One of the first things I remember was lemon meringue pie. My mum wasn't really interested in baking, but she did make that. I also remember my sixth birthday at a holiday camp and having a shop-bought Battenberg cake with candles stuck in it.

What's your guilty food pleasure?

I really love eating crisps. I could eat crisps all day long, but I'm trying to wean myself off them and on to something a bit healthier, so I'm really getting into beef jerky.

If you could invite anyone past or present around for tea, who would it be and what would you bake?

Mark Gonzales, the godfather of skateboarding. He was huge in the 1980s and '90s. He's from New York, so I'd probably bake him jalapeño pretzels, I think he'd like those.

If you could bake only one thing, what would it be?

Sourdough. I made a cracking one the other week that was the best I've ever had in my life. If I could have that every day, I'd be happy.

When you're not baking, how do you relax?

I was a runner for years, but I'm not able to run now due to a running-specific injury. Skateboarding, I'm big into that. Me and my mates go to skate parks all over the southeast. Then, of course, we go to the pub. I also like painting.

Who do you like to bake for?

The guys at the fire station. There's 12 of us there, and most cakes portion nicely into 12. They've started asking for certain fancy things now, though the other week it was flapjacks. Also, they'll eat anything, those lads!

What's the one piece of fire safety advice you'd give would-be bakers?

Always have a smoke alarm fitted, and check it regularly.

What are your five favourite bakes?

Sourdough bread, jalapeño pretzels, millionaire's shortbread, homemade pizza, and orange and passion fruit cake.

What's your worst baking disaster?

I decided to make some macarons for my audition bake. My first batch went in at 8am and I just couldn't get them to work. The very last batch came out at 10pm and were all right, which was lucky as I had no more raw ingredients left and all the shops were shut. It's the pressure. If you're making them for yourself at home, they'd turn out fine.

What's the most surprising, unusual or interesting thing in your cupboard?

Citric acid monohydrate, which is used to make elderflower cordial. I bought it but never got round to making the cordial, and then had to throw away the elderflowers I picked.

What's your favourite kitchen gadget?

I suppose I should say the electric mixer my wife's bridesmaids bought us as a wedding present. But actually I've got this really good spatula I found in my mum's kitchen. It must be about 30 years old, but it's great at getting right into the corners.

Describe your kitchen at home.

It's tiny. I can touch all four walls when standing in the middle. There's hardly any workspace. The sink is always full up, as we've no dishwasher and I use everything when I bake. It looks very nice and it's got great tiling, as I did that!

What's your favourite ingredient to work with?

I'm much more a savoury person than sweet. I really like working with different types of flour, like rye or wholemeal, and especially strong plain white flour. You can mix anything with it and use that as a building block for big flavours.

Do you keep a recipe notebook?

No, not at all. I take the worst notes ever! I've got the notes from when I was developing recipes for the show, and often it's just a word on a page – it infuriates me. I'd just end up doodling a picture of a skateboard or something.

What's your party trick?

I don't know really. I always thought I was good at break-dancing, but I'm not.

Tell us one thing about yourself that will surprise us.

I'm descended from Tom Cribb, a bare-knuckle boxer who became Heavyweight Champion of the World in 1811.

What did it feel like when you found out you'd been selected for *Bake Off* 2015?

When the phone went to tell me I'd got on the show, I was actually in the bath in the French Alps. I'd applied as a bit of a joke, so I couldn't believe it. I was probably more daunted than excited.

What's your favourite *Bake Off* moment from a previous series?

Luis' biscuit George and the Dragon. The way it just slotted together, incredible.

Who's your favourite past baker and why?

The person I really liked was Richard from last year – you know, with the pencil behind his ear. He's what made me apply. When you see someone like that you think, 'Yeah, I can do this.' He's the sort of person you could have a chat with down the pub. He's an everyman and I can relate to him.

YOUR BAKES FROM HOME

Sometimes the hardest task for the bakers in the tent isn't their mountainous Showstoppers or beloved Signature Bakes – it's diving into the unknown with the Technical Challenges. The bakers could be asked to create anything from florentines to floating islands. At home, and perhaps under a little less pressure, you have given these recipes a crack too. Here are some of your efforts.

Technical Challenges
▼▼▼▼▼▼▼▼▼▼▼▼

FONDANT FANCIES

As baked by the Finalists of 2012

1. Made by Fee from Newton Aycliffe

Great chocolate finishing touch, Fee. Her tip is to chill the cake fully before applying the fondant topping.

2. Made by Hannah from Tadcaster

This is a supersized version of the family favourite. The humungous lemon buttercream fondant topping looks pretty fancy to us.

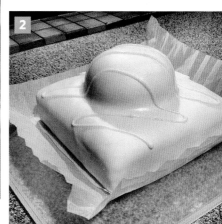

CHARLOTTE ROYALE

Baked by the 2013 Quarter-finalists

3. Made by Lynsey from Nuneaton

Lynsey's attempt at this tricky dish is very professional-looking. The Swiss roll slices are packed tightly together and, as a result, there's isn't even a hint of custard leakage.

4. Made by Eliza from London

Another fine stab at the pudding. Topped with strawberries for extra panache.

SWEDISH PRINCESS TORTE

As seen in 2014's European Cake Week

7. Made by Rachel from Glasgow

A very difficult cake to create, and Rachel has done herself proud. The smooth green marzipan overlay is free from bumps and creases. As the Swedish would say, 'Perfekt!'

FRAISIER CAKE

Seen in the 2012 Quarter-final

8. Made by Liz from Gerrards Cross

A great alternative for a birthday cake, this layered lemon sponge and chocolate mousse creation looks really tempting. It's supported all the way around with upright strawberries and decorated with chocolate hearts.

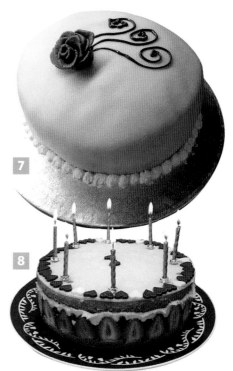

5. Made by Jo from Moreton-in-Marsh

Jo intended to make a Charlotte Royale and got as far as the first stage – the Swiss roll. Then she got side-tracked by the arrival of her in-laws, ran out of time for the second stage, and they ended up eating the cake with a cup of tea! Better luck next time, Jo.

HAND-RAISED PIE

Seen in 2012's Pie Week

6. Made by Lauren from Wallingford

A hand-raised pie is made using hot-water crust and a nifty little kitchen tool known as a 'pie dolly' to shape it. Lauren's pie is filled with chicken and apricot, and we think it looks pretty special.

9. Made by Hannah from Macclesfield

This version comes complete with a Jackson Pollock-esque icing design for that extra bit of class. Frances would be proud.

APRICOT COURONNE

As baked in 2013's Sweet Dough Week

10. Made by Marie from Stalbridge

We reckon this sweet dough creation would've given the class of 2013 a run for their money. Marie said she had great fun making it, and that it tasted divine.

BATTENBERG

As baked in 2011's Cake Week

11. Made by Ben from London

Hats off to Ben, this Battenberg would certainly get the Mary Berry seal of approval. A great shape, and maintaining neat squares on slicing, this is a teatime treat we certainly wouldn't turn down.

Blackbirds, Eels and Dwarves: history's most unusual pie fillings

In times past, a pie was part surprise gift, part jack-in-the-box. Until you opened it, you couldn't be quite sure what was inside. It was this sense of anticipation that show-off hosts loved to create, entertaining their unsuspecting guests with pie fillings of the most unusual kind. And the most unusual surely has to be a dwarf.

❖

Jeffery Hudson (1619–*c*.1682) was just seven years old and a mere 45 cm high when he was presented to King Charles I and his teenage bride, Queen Henrietta Maria, at a banquet given by the Duke of Buckingham.

Dressed in a miniature suit of armour, he was placed inside a baked pie case, which was carried into the hall and placed before the queen. Everyone held their breath, then the little boy sprang out of the crust and did a dance on the table. The young queen couldn't believe her eyes, and Jeffery remained in her company until the English Civil War in 1642.

Medieval cooks were masters of pastry-making, creating huge pies for royal feasts, often richly gilded and decorated with scenes designed to flatter honoured guests. In many cases the pastry wasn't even meant to be eaten, but was used to keep the filling moist and secure. Guests would simply remove the lid and eat the contents with a spoon.

Other odd pie fillings from history include lampreys, a fish that resembles a particularly ugly eel – slimy, jawless and with a single nostril on top. Despite their unappealing appearance, they were considered a delicacy at the royal court, and often baked into pies. Henry I loved them, and is said to have died in 1135 from complications brought on by 'a surfeit of lampreys', though it was more likely to be food poisoning.

The tradition of huge royal pies continued until quite recently. On Christmas Day 1857, the royal family sat down to a game pie so large that it took four footmen to carry it into the dining room.

Perhaps the most famous unusual pie filling is the 'four and twenty blackbirds' that were 'baked in a pie'. This nursery rhyme first appeared in print in the 1700s, but live animals were used as entertainment at the table long before then. The chef Robert May, author of *The Accomplisht Cook* (1660), gives a recipe 'where lifting first the lid off one pye, out skip some frogs, which make the ladies to skip and shreek'.

STARGAZEY PIE

The village of Mousehole (pronounced 'mow-zul') in Cornwall is the home of Stargazey pie, which has a fish filling arranged in a most unusual way. The fish are placed so that their heads poke though the pastry lid and gaze up at the stars – hence the name of the pie. Legend has it that one winter in the sixteenth century, the people of Mousehole were facing starvation due to bad weather. Only one brave fisherman, Tom Bawcock, braved the rough seas. The catch he brought back was baked into a pie that the whole town shared. His heroic deeds are celebrated every 23 December in the town to this day.

The first female cookery writer

Hannah Wolley or Woolley (b. 1623) was the first woman to earn a living from writing cookery books. She published four of them, aimed at the female servants of aristocratic families, but also those lower down the social scale. Her recipes included artichoke pie and oyster pie, as well as home remedies such as 'plague water'. This distillation of sage and other herbs mixed with pepper and treacle was far from delicious, but claimed to offer protection against the pox and measles.

BRITAIN'S BEST PIE

The annual search for the best pie in Britain takes place in March at the British Pie Awards in Melton Mowbray, Leicestershire. Nearly a thousand pies are entered each year, in categories such as Best Pork Pie, Best Vegetarian Pie and even Best Football Pie. Presumably, if the last of these is a draw, it goes to extra time and then penalties.

BAKERS V JUDGES

IT TAKES A brave, or perhaps foolhardy, kind of baker to challenge the heavyweights of the baking world – Paul Hollywood and Mary Berry. But once in a while a hungry amateur comes along who fancies their chances with these seasoned pros. At such times, the tent can feel like a boxing ring, with baking jabs and uppercuts flying around amongst the bunting. But have any of these kitchen contenders managed to land a knock-out blow?

WHEN THE (OVEN) GLOVES COME OFF

BREADLOCK!
(2014)

VS

In the red corner:
NANCY, aka 'THE KNEADER'

In the blue corner:
PAUL 'THE STICKLER' HOLLYWOOD

DING DING! Seconds out...

Paul Hollywood has made a career from baking perfect bread, so in Advanced Dough Week, when he heard that scrappy new girl on the block Nancy planned to prove her Lincolnshire Plum Bread Signature Bake in the microwave, he immediately went on the offensive: 'It's a dangerous thing to do,' he warned ominously. 'It'll destroy the protein structure,' he jabbed. But Nancy, never one to back down from a challenge, microwaved her dough not once, but twice, during baking. Forget 'Ding ding,

seconds out' – for Nancy it was more 'Ping ping, seconds out… and leave to stand for a minute.' But would the microwave trick pulverise Nancy's precious proteins and prove 'Stickler' Hollywood right?

TOUGHEST BLOW: 'It's the size of a Labrador!' Sue commented unhelpfully about Nancy's oversized dough, doing nothing to bolster her confidence.

RESULT: Nancy is literally saved by the bell, and her microwaved Plum Bread wins by a knock-out! Paul suspected the proteins had been destroyed and that the bake was a little underdone. However, on tasting it, his lack of criticism, if not glowing praise, gave her hope as he admitted, 'It's got a good structure.' It was surprise supporter Mary who finally gave Nancy the upper hand. 'I think it tastes absolutely scrumptious!' she glowed, giving Paul no option but to throw in the tea towel.

tent; he could out-punch Hollywood too. 'I've a point to prove now,' he said, with a faint quiver of fear in his voice as he set about creating his Passion Fruit Mille-feuille. Could Glenn's inverted pastry technique knock Paul for six?

TOUGHEST BLOW: Paul didn't pull his punches: 'They look awful!' (Ouch!) 'They look hideous!' (Ooof!) 'They're a mess!' (Grnff!) 'They look like they've been dropped!' (Mummy!)

RESULT: Paul came out the winner, a proud champion of traditional pastry-making methods. Glenn went down fighting, but his duff puff was the last dish he served in the tent. Ever the gentleman, he admitted graceful defeat, collected his winnings (plenty of dough) and left the tent.

FISTIPUFFS!
(2013)

In the red corner:

GLENN aka 'LAST MAN STANDING'

In the blue corner:

PAUL 'THE LAMINATOR' HOLLYWOOD

DING DING! Seconds out…

Glenn, the final man in the tent during Pastry Week, decided that the best way of flooring the judges was to use some highly unorthodox tactics. For his Showstopper of three miniature pastries, he chose to make puff pastry by folding the dough into the butter, not the other way round, a decision that so rattled Paul, he saw a red mist descending. 'I'm not convinced. I think doing it the traditional way gets you extremely good results,' he told Glenn.

But Glenn wasn't going to let Paul force him onto the ropes. He'd seen off every other man in that

THE GINGE-OFF!
(2010)

In the red corner:

RUTH aka 'BRAVE SPICE'

In the blue corner:

PAUL 'THE MEAN MACHINE' HOLLYWOOD &
MARY 'DEATH STARE' BERRY

DING DING! Seconds out...

When Ruth boldly announced that her final Signature Bake was to be a Mint, Ginger and Blackberry Cupcake, she found herself being stared down by the judges. The unusual combination alone was enough to unbalance Paul, who believed that the three flavours would fight each other. Ruth's further admission that she was using not powdered ginger but fresh really got Mary's hackles up. This was shaping up to be a bare-knuckle bake...

Ruth, however, was full of confidence in her recipe – a family favourite – and determined to slug it out.

The judges circled the controversial cake cautiously, gingerly even. Would the flavour collision prove Ruth's secret weapon in what could be her last bout in the baking ring?

TOUGHEST BLOW: Mary went in with a swift uppercut: 'I've never seen fresh ginger grated into a cake and now I know why. It doesn't really work. I didn't enjoy it.'

RESULT: Ruth lost the bout, all stemming (sorry) from her love of ginger. Mary and Paul were right – when three strong flavours collide, only one will dominate. Feisty Ruth didn't admit defeat, though: 'It was right, it is right and I wouldn't change it!' Attagirl!

ART ATTACK!
(2013)

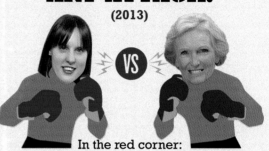

In the red corner:

FRANCES aka 'DEADLY DESIGNER'

In the blue corner:

MARY 'CRUSHER' BERRY

DING DING! Seconds out...

It was a showdown that had been building in the tent for weeks. Frances' elaborate designs and flights of fancy were gaining her quite a reputation as the baker who put the 'art' into 'tart'. So when her Pastry Week pitch for the savoury canapé Signature Bake seemed to focus more on her presentation than the flavours, Mary swiftly launched her attack. 'Now, I hope we're not having rabbits all around the outside, or flowers,' she battered into Frances. 'We're concentrating on the canapés.'

Frances was forced to do some fancy footwork, ducking and weaving and reassuring the judges that she was planning to produce a great bake. Would she follow through and knock them out with a double whammy of design and deliciousness?

TOUGHEST BLOW: When Paul asked for 'substance over style' for a change, Frances came back with some fighting talk: 'I'm aiming to put the style on the substance.' (Pow!)

RESULT: Frances' Vegetable-themed Canapés were a triumph. 'You've cracked it!' Mary conceded, while Paul offered the victor a gallant handshake. Soon afterwards, Frances battered all the other bakers on her way to being crowned Bake Off champion, winning the competition in style (and substance).

MATCH THE BAKER TO THE BAKE

CHETNA   LUIS   BECA   ROBERT   FRANCES   NORMAN   CATHRYN

1. A butternut squash and pecan 'cheese' cake. Who came up with this clever cake?

2. Only a baker with a sideline in science could produce a Doctor Who themed biscuit scene...

3. This chocolate, peanut butter and pumpkin pie was a labour of love for this young parent, always nervous of the judges' verdict...

4. It's a banoffee traybake and a game of Jenga... what kind of baking genius could come up with such a thing?

5. This 'Pieffel Tower' was topped with a (very strong) lavender meringue pie. Ooh la la!

6. This cardamom, pistachio and coffee swiss roll was a delight, from a baker who knew their flavours well...

7. This was a final showstopper pièce montée, inspired by their Cheshire hometown.

ARE YOU A BAKING BOFFIN?

Think you know your Dorset nob from your rustic cob, or your cheese soufflé from your crème brûlée? See how you get on with this 'baker's dozen' of baking questions...

1. What's the difference between a cake and a biscuit?

☞ Cakes go hard when they are stale, whereas biscuits go soft. And that's official! This is why Jaffa cakes are, in fact, biscuits.

2. If you asked for the Italian dessert Tiramisu, but using the English translation, what would you ask for?

☞ 'Pick me up'. It's the coffee in this simple Italian dessert that is said to give a lift. It's a modern creation, dating from the 1960s, and may have been an evolution of an early dish called Zuppa Inglese, literally 'English soup', but actually an Italian take on trifle. Unlike the original layers of custard and sherry-soaked sponges, Tiramisu has coffee-soaked sponge fingers layered with whipped mascarpone and eggs.

3. Why do we blow out candles on a birthday cake?

☞ It started out as a religious custom in ancient Greece. Worshippers would offer cakes to Artemis, goddess of chastity, placing candles on them possibly in the belief that the smoke would carry their prayers up to the gods. This is why we continue to make a silent wish before blowing out candles on a birthday cake.

4. Where do Danish Pastries come from?

☞ Austria. In 1850, bakers in Denmark went on strike, so the bakery owners brought in highly skilled Austrian bakers to do their work. These bakers were unfamiliar with Danish bakes, so instead they baked their classic pastries from Austria. In Denmark today, the word for 'pastry' is wienerbrød (Viennese bread), Vienna being the capital of Austria.

5. What dessert features a 'thousand leaves'?

☞ Mille-feuille. The layers of puff pastry used in this classic French dessert are said to number a thousand, but let's do the maths. In Mastering the Art of French Cooking Julia Child recommends folding the butter and dough into thirds and rolling out again, before giving it half a turn and repeating this six times. If you do this, you'll technically end up with 729 laminations or layers, though in fact most will merge during the cooking process. Add to this that most mille-feuilles have three layers of puff pastry between the fillings and the total layer count is a mind-boggling 2187. Of course, 'deux mille cent quatre-vingt-sept feuille' is a bit of mouthful to say! Perhaps we should take a leaf out of the Americans' book and simply call them Napoleons.

6. What's the main difference between an Eccles Cake and a Chorley Cake?

☞ Both are flattened fruit cakes that originate from Lancashire towns, but Eccles Cakes are made from puff pastry whereas Chorley Cakes use shortcrust. Eccles Cakes are sometimes called 'squashed fly pies' because the currants in them are said to resemble flies.

7. What is the difference between currants, raisins and sultanas?

☞ Currants are dried, seedless red grapes that become almost black after drying. These grapes were originally cultivated in southern Greece, and the word 'currant' is a corruption of 'Corinth', an ancient city in that part of the world. Raisins are dried white grapes, usually the muscatel variety. They become dark brown when dried and, unlike currants, can soak up other flavours, particularly alcohol. Sultanas are a specific type of white grape, namely Thompson Sultana. They dry to a golden colour rather than dark brown, and tend to be plumper, sweeter and juicier than raisins.

8. What do Brazil nuts, cashew nuts, walnuts, peanuts and coconuts have in common?

☛ They're not nuts. Brazils and cashews are seeds, while the others are something called drupes. What's more, Brazil isn't even the biggest producer of Brazil nuts – that title goes to Bolivia next door.

9. According to folklore, which bake is considered to be lucky when taken aboard a ship?

☛ A hot cross bun. Having religious connotations, it's said to protect you from being shipwrecked.

10. How well do you know your European bakes? Time to find out. Which of these is not a European cake, pastry, bread or biscuit?
Speculoos ▪ Baklava ▪ Piparkakut ▪ Tiropita ▪ Eekhoorntjesbrood ▪ Oliebollen ▪ Spanakopita

☛ Eekhoorntjesbrood. It's actually the Dutch word for porcini mushrooms, though it translates literally as 'little squirrels' bread'. The others are as follows:

Speculoos – a spiced shortcrust biscuit from the Netherlands

Baklava – a filo pastry dessert filled with chopped nuts and honey from Turkey

Piparkakut – gingerbread biscuits from Finland

Tiropita – a cheese-filled pastry from Greece

Oliebollen – a type of doughnut from Belgium and the Netherlands

Spanakopita – a spinach-and-feta-filled pastry from Greece

Wirthsleute

11. What type of cake did this German traditional costume inspire?

☛ The Black Forest Gateau. The red pompoms on the hat inspired the whole cherries used in the dessert, the white blouse the cream, and the dark dress the chocolate cake. Today the costume is worn only on ceremonial occasions or special holidays in the Black Forest. Unmarried girls' hats are topped with red pompoms, while married women have black ones.

12. Where are these two pasties from?

☛ If you thought Cornwall, you're only half right. The one on the left with the crimped seal across the top is considered a Devon pasty, while the one with the crimp along the side is a Cornish pasty. The Cornish version now has PGI (Protected Geographical Indication) status, meaning that the genuine article has to be made in that county and have the familiar 'D' shape.

13. How do you make a Swiss roll?

☛ Push him down a hill!

RETRO BAKES: booze, biscuits and the Black Forest

In the 1960s and 1970s, Britain turned its back on centuries of suety boiled puddings and went mad for fancy European bakes, while new technologies, such as home freezers, allowed busy mums to give the family or dinner guests something special. Here's our retro round-up of some familiar favourites.

Vol-au-vents, Quiche Lorraine and Black Forest Gateau

Nothing puts the kitsch into kitchen more than these retro bakes straight from the 1970s. Vol-au-vents (which means 'windblown' in French, a nod to their lightness) are pastry shells stuffed with a filling. Of course with typical British gusto, most of us made them as heavy as a cricket ball. Quiche Lorraine is considered a classic French dish, and found its way on to many British picnic blankets in the 1970s. In fact, we've had egg-filled tarts and flans like this in England since the fourteenth century. Finally, as the name suggests, Black Forest Gateau heralds from Germany, where, like beer, there are strict rules about the ingredients that can be used. The most important is the liberal application of kirsch, the local cherry liqueur.

Boozy bakes

In fact, there was lots of alcohol sloshing about in 1970s kitchens. Other popular boozy bakes included Rum Babas. If you got one of these at a dinner party, your host was definitely a Star Baker. Made from enriched brioche dough, they were introduced to France in

the eighteenth century by the exiled Polish king Stanisław Leszczyński. He was a keen reader of the folk tale collection called *A Thousand and One Nights*, and named the dish after Ali Baba, the hero of one of the stories. So, it's a French dough soaked in West Indian alcohol, invented by a Polish king and named after a fictional Arabian hero. Got it!

Simpler stuff

Of course, the likes of Black Forest Gateau and Rum Baba were fancy baking, not everyday events. Most teatime puddings featured simple shop-bought bakes, such as Arctic Roll. When you were eight years old, few things were better than sponge cake wrapped around ice cream.

But why was the sponge always soft, despite just coming out of the freezer? Years later, the reason was revealed. Apparently, the baking process drives all the moisture out of the sponge, meaning no ice crystals can form to freeze it hard. Sadly for younger readers, the Arctic Roll was discontinued in the 1980s.

Biscuit blasts from the past

In the 1970s, every house had a biscuit barrel, from which kids would grab Jammy Dodgers, Party Rings, Chocolate Bourbons or Pink Wafers to enjoy with a glass of milk and Blue Peter on the telly.

Many of these biscuits were invented in Victorian times when, oddly, they were marketed as slimming aids. Mass-production saw them move from being a luxury to an everyday treat that's still with us today. Indeed, in the UK we eat more biscuits than any other country in Europe, with the average household dunking, nibbling and crunching its way through 103 packets of biscuits a year – champions!

DIGESTIVE BISCUITS

- Three digestive biscuits contain as much salt as a packet of crisps.
- A staggering 4.4 million digestives are eaten in the UK every day, most of which are dunked in tea.

THE GREAT BRITISH BAKE OFF
Hall Of Fame

Richard's Pesto Pinwheel (2014)

MARY: 'It looks very neat. I love the pesto.'

PAUL: 'You've baked it really well, actually. The flavour and the texture works extremely well. That's a very, very nice loaf.'

Martha's Ski Village Scene (2014)

MARY: 'As soon as you bite into it, beautifully crisp, the coffee taste hits you.'

PAUL: 'It's ingenious and creative, well thought through.'

Christine's Shortbread Bavarian Clock Tower (2013)

PAUL: 'Very cute. It's a good, strong structure. All the flavours are good. The texture's good, the bake's good, the look of them is good – excellent.'

MARY: 'I think that's stunning. You have made something you could put on a tea party table and everybody would have a decent piece of shortbread.'

Iain's Wild West 3D Biscuit Scene (2014)

MARY: 'It's supporting itself, everything is standing up. Nice snap with the oatmeal. Quite sweet. Good crunch.'

PAUL: 'It's a nice biscuit that. It tastes good. I think you've done well. Your flavours are distinct and sharp enough and then the display is well thought out and very well executed.'

James' Smoky Cayenne, Cumin and Chilli Crackers (2012)

MARY: 'They are beautifully crisp. Difficult to achieve. Well done for getting them so wafer-thin and full of flavour.'

PAUL: 'I do like the flavour, I like the seeds as well, the little bit of fire in there as well from the cayenne.'

Beca's Tiered Macaron and Sugar Dough Biscuit Centrepiece (2013)

MARY: 'I think it's fun. It would be great for a little girl's party.'

PAUL: 'The macarons are exceptional.'

YOUR BAKES FROM HOME

In 2013 the climax for the bakers came with a mammoth task – to design and bake a show-stopping wedding cake. Frances, Kimberley and Ruby all rose to the challenge, although it was the *Midsummer Night's Dream* cake by Frances that really brought the curtain down, sealing the deal for her to take the *Bake Off* crown. Your own attempts at creating the perfect cake for a special day are just as winning.

Wedding Cakes

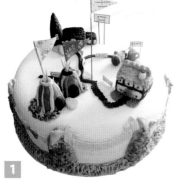

1

3. Birch Tree
Made by An from Belgium

This wedding cake is shaped like the trunk of a birch tree, complete with romantic carving on the icing 'bark'. An made it for her own wedding!

3

1. 'Wedstival' Cake
Made by Fran from Swindon

The design on this cake is perfect for a festival-themed big day, complete with teepees, champagne and a miniature glass of ale.

2. Twin Decks
Made by Danielle from Great Bentley

Going by this very personal wedding cake designed in the shape of vinyl mixing decks, we're guessing Samantha and Jason are no strangers to a night out. A lot of hard work has gone in to this musical one-off.

4

5. Groom on a Bike!
Made by Lois from Redditch

The inspiration for this wedding cake comes from the groom's love of mountain biking, while the traditional elements were requested by the bride. The path is made from mini chocolate buttons. Let's hope the bike doesn't get a puncture en route.

2

4. Chinese Dragon Cake
Made by Michelle from Wootton

According to Michelle, the dragons are moulded out of rice crispies and marshmallow so as not to add too much weight to the finished cake. This is a clever, original design.

5

10. Lemon and Blackberry Cake
Made by Louise from Hampshire

A three-layered cake of lemon sponge, buttercream and fresh blackberries. We love the extra touch of the surrounding cupcakes, and the addition of photos is a great idea.

6. Chocolate Paste Cake
Made by Chris from Kenley

Swathes of white chocolate paste give this cake a really sumptuous finish that looks soft to the touch. It's finished with homemade sugar roses.

7. Butterfly Cake
Made by Trudie from Southampton

A classic tiered design is given an elegant twist with ornate edible butterflies. Made by Trudie for a friend's wedding, the layers of cake under the icing are fruit, vanilla Madeira and chocolate fudge.

8. Naked Wedding Cake
Made by Liz from Buckinghamshire

This eye-catching bake grabs attention by stripping things right back. Losing the layers of icing gives this cake a pretty, unfussy air of cool. Stuffed full of fresh fruit and cream, it's proof that sometimes less is more.

9. Vintage Style
Made by Louise from Ireland

For her classic wedding design, Louise has used icing with a pink and purple theme above layers of lemon zest sponge, buttercream and a hazelnut and chocolate biscuit cake. Vibrant and delicious!

11. Lace Cake
Made by Denise from Malvern

The hand-piped lace decoration on this wedding cake is amazing. Under the icing the cake is actually a gluten-free lemon-drizzle sponge and a nut-free apricot and cherry cake.

12. Suitcase Cake
Made by Liz from Sheffield

Throwing tradition out of the window, this chocolate wedding cake has two tiers cleverly designed to look like honeymoon suitcases. Hopefully it was packed full of flavour.

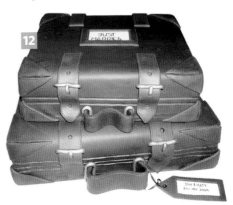

NADIYA

What got you into baking?

I think I kind of stumbled upon it when I got married. Growing up, we never really used the oven. In our culture, there's no such thing as dessert. But at school my home economics teacher said, 'You're actually quite good.' Soon I was staying behind at lunchtime to learn more, and the obsession started from there. When I got married and got my own oven, it dawned on me that I could bake.

Tell us about your earliest food memory.

My dad and uncle are both chefs, so we grew up enjoying good food. My dad would cook half a sheep in a pot and say, 'You're all coming round,' and 40 of us – family, neighbours, friends – would all gather to eat.

Have your kids caught the baking bug?

Yes, all three of them can bake. They're quite good, as they've watched me for years. My daughter watches cake tutorials on the Internet and picks up these little details. She's definitely got the bug.

Can you give us a great idea for children's party food?

Melt-in-the-middle cake pops: I put something gooey in the middle, such as jam. Or how about a piñata cake that they can smash to get the chocolates from inside? Failing that, anything with popping candy.

What's your guilty food pleasure?

It's anything with salted caramel. I could have it with rice, with carrots, with curry. I try and get it into everything. My family say, 'You can't put salted caramel in everything,' and I say, 'Yes you can!'

If you could invite anyone past or present around for tea, who would it be and what would you bake?

I'd invite Paul and Mary. It would be so nice to bake for them in the comfort of my home without that feeling of being under pressure.

And what would you bake them?

Anything I failed in the tent. I'd present it and say, 'Look, I can do this. I just got nervous before!'

If you could bake only one thing, what would it be?

Brioche. It's the most comforting, delicious bread. Much as I try to stay away from it, it's one of my favourite things to bake.

When you're not baking, how do you relax?

Running, that's how I relax. I do about 12 miles most days. In the past I was two stone heavier. My daughter's five years old now, so I can't say it's 'baby weight' any more – running is a must.

Who do you like to bake for?

My family, though anyone who'll eat it, to be honest. My brothers and sisters are awful bakers, but they're good at eating. They're the ones I love to feed, and I'm always the one who turns up with dessert.

What are your five favourite bakes?

Brioche, profiteroles, chocolate swap cake (something I created), quiches and my duck and orange pie.

What's your worst baking disaster?

I've had so many. I once promised someone I'd make them macarons, so I started at 8am, thinking I'd get them wrong once. By 10pm I'd got them wrong seven times! I was in a foetal position in front of the oven. But by 1am I'd made my eighth batch, and they were perfect.

What's the most surprising, unusual or interesting thing in your cupboard?

Mulberry molasses. It's the most unusual, bizarre flavour, and I've used it in lots of savoury and sweet bakes. I really like it now.

What's your favourite kitchen gadget?

My ice cream-maker. I've had it for six months. Homemade ice cream is way better than the shop-bought stuff.

Describe your kitchen at home.

It's the focal point of our home, our main living space, and we spend a lot of time here. We got to the point where we had to buy new freezers and put them in the shed. I've a fan-assisted oven, and my electric mixer has pride of place.

What's your favourite ingredient to work with?

Right now I really like working with halal gelatine. As a Muslim, I've had to avoid things like marshmallows and jelly sweets because gelatine is made from pork. But I got some very expensive halal gelatine and it's totally changed my baking. It means I can make bakes like pannacotta, or marshmallows.

Do you keep a recipe notebook?

I do, and I've had one for years. I've one version which has recipes for me, and one with 'simple' recipes, which is for my husband for when I'm out or away.

What did it feel like when you found out you'd been selected for *Bake Off* 2015?

Surreal, as it's quite a long process, and you almost convince yourself you're not going to get in. I hadn't prepared myself at all for the fact I'd get it. When I was told, I just screamed down the phone.

What's your favourite *Bake Off* moment from a previous series?

Ian's Baked Alaska was fun, though it's cruel to say that was my favourite bit. My 2014 highlight, though, was Nancy winning, despite Richard being the favourite.

Who's your favourite past baker and why?

Nancy was the one I wanted to win, but one of my favourite bakers was Kate from Series Five. Nobody can rock pink highlights like she can! She was fun, and her baking was cool. I think it was Week Seven that she left, and I was so sad.

PAUL

What got you into baking?

When I was growing up, there was lots of baking around, and as a kid you watch things. I joined the army at 18 and was always looking for ways to spice up the ration pack. Later children came along, and I stopped for a while. Then, in 1994, I did a friend's wedding cake, two tiers with flowers down the side. I saw *Bake Off* and thought, 'I can do that, but they don't let people like me on.'

Tell us about your earliest food memory.

I can remember the lemon meringue pies my dad enjoyed, and homemade lollies, that sort of thing. For things I've made myself, one of the first was a carrot cake.

What's your guilty food pleasure?

I'm a meat eater. I love lamb chops and I regularly buy a big bag of them from the farm shop and keep them in the freezer. I'm not really a great sweet person. I make ice cream, but it's for the kids. Having said that, I can eat wine gums by the packet.

If you could invite anyone past or present around for tea, who would it be and what would you bake?

Sir David Attenborough, because I love nature and really respect him. I'd love to hear about his exploits and adventures over the years, from the Galapagos Islands to the jungles of Indonesia. I think I'd make us a traditional sticky toffee pudding with caramel sauce and Madagascan vanilla ice cream.

If you could bake only one thing, what would it be?

Bread. It comes in so many forms, you can make a whole meal from it, and there's such a variety.

When you're not baking, how do you relax?

I like to read. I've a sea kayak in the garage and we go to Pembrokeshire when the weather's nice. In the past, I'd put a couple of rods in the back and we'd cast off for mackerel or bass, just gently paddling along.

Who do you like to bake for?

My kids and my wife. They love it when I bake. I like to bake for colleagues at work too. They do appreciate it as whenever I take something in, it's all gone in a flash.

How important is order and discipline in baking?

The type of roles I've had since I was 18, whether it's in the army or prison service, are all about discipline. I won't just get stuck into a recipe - instead I have to make a list. I'm a list person. It's the same with baking and sugarcraft. You don't want to throw it all in and hope for the best.

What are your five favourite bakes?

A bloomer (I make one most weekends), iced fingers, lemon cake, mince pies (can't do without them at Christmas) and Cornish pasties made properly with skirt meat.

What's your worst baking disaster?

I was trying to do a type of fancy layered cake called a dacquoise. The recipe called for pistachio paste. I didn't have any, so tried to improvise and make my own. It looked like mush. It was disgusting. Another disaster was biscotti. They were like bricks and would have kept a dentist in business for years. I also once put vanilla in rhubarb and it was horrible – didn't go at all.

What's the most surprising, unusual or interesting thing in your cupboard?

Green peppercorns. I had an ice cream recipe that called for them, and it worked! I didn't know you could get such things: you put them in a pestle and mortar and bash them up. I also make orange-infused sugar for a syrup I put on cakes. Oh, and some chocolate-coated popping candy! I've also got something called isomalt [a healthy substitute for sugar]. You dust food colouring powder over it and bake to make an edible stained-glass 'window'.

What's your favourite kitchen gadget?

My oven because without it, I'm stuffed! Everything goes in it. However, the item I probably use the most is a spatula.

Describe your kitchen at home.

It's not a large kitchen, about 10 x 14ft. We have a big, American-style fridge that I moved out to the garage, and in the space I built a dedicated baking bench, with another oven to the side of it. This is where I do all my baking. Now my son has gone to university, I've also converted his bedroom upstairs into my sugarwork room.

What's your favourite ingredient to work with?

I really like dough. I don't use the mixer to make it, and think using a bread-maker is cheating! I just get the ingredients in a bowl and work it for a good five to ten minutes. I follow Paul's advice and use oil to 'dust' the bench.

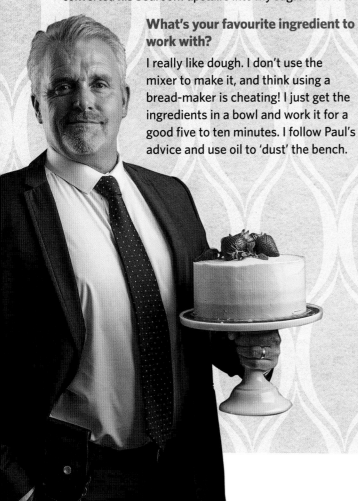

Do you keep a recipe notebook?

I've got a bamboo box with index cards inside, and keep recipes in there. But I'm moving more towards saving things on my tablet now.

What's your party trick?

I can make a recorder out of a carrot and play a tune on it.

Tell us one thing about yourself that will surprise us.

I can sew! Years ago I bought my wife a sewing machine and she didn't even thread cotton on the thing, so I did. I've since used it to make pillowcases and duvets. I can also put zips in.

What did it feel like when you found out you'd been selected for *Bake Off* 2015?

I was very surprised. My wife had previously said, 'I think you're going to get on it,' but I wasn't convinced. When I did, I thought, 'Oh dear, what have I let myself in for?'

How did you prepare for *Bake Off*?

I read lots and lots of books to get ideas. I've watched it since Series One, so I knew all the categories – biscuits, breads, pies and so on – went through all of them for research. I also looked at a flavour thesaurus to get ideas for flavour combinations. Finally, I did lots of practice!

What's your favourite *Bake Off* moment from a previous series?

When Jordan, the IT guy from Series Five, made the Godzilla scene. I liked that and he was a real character.

Who's your favourite past baker and why?

Richard from the last series. He was a nice bloke – a builder and a plasterer. He was consistent and good, and I liked the pencil behind the ear. I didn't mind applying because he'd done it.

HISTORY

WASTE NOT WANT NOT: uses for stale bread

Every day in Britain we throw away approximately 24 million slices of bread.* If all those slices were to be lined up next to each other, they'd form a loaf around 149 miles long! Perhaps we could take a leaf from the past, when bread was so important that not a scrap was wasted, giving rise to some classic dishes that can only really be made with stale bread.

Let's begin in Italy, and in particular with the people of Tuscany. Tuscan bread stays soft for a matter of hours before going stale. On the plus side, it then lasts for ages. In this state it's used as a thickener in ribollita, a vegetable and bean soup; and in panzanella, a summery dish that combines onions, tomatoes and basil with toasted stale bread – great for soaking up the juices. Both dishes have a long history stretching back to the Middle Ages. Older still is a dish of slightly stale bread soaked in eggs and then fried. The French call this *pain perdu* (lost bread), while in the UK it's known as French toast, but versions have existed in one form or another since the fourth century.

The Spanish and Portuguese have *migas* (literally 'crumbs'), which is simply breadcrumbs fried in spicy oil. They also have romesco sauce, made with nuts and roasted peppers and thickened with breadcrumbs.

Here in Britain we also know a thing or two about turning stale bread into delicious dishes. We have the classic bread and butter pudding, which gives new life to old bread by combining it with beaten egg and milk, spices, sugar and dried fruit. And then there's treacle tart, a pastry case containing a mixture of breadcrumbs and golden syrup. Savoury British dishes of the past included 'buttered crumbs' – breadcrumbs fried in butter and traditionally served with game; while bread sauce – a mixture of breadcrumbs, onion, milk and spices – is still popular with roast turkey.

Unfortunately, modern baking methods mean that the average supermarket loaf tends to go mouldy rather than stale, and there's nothing appetising to be made out of that. Instead, buy or, even better, make real bread. It lasts longer, and if by chance you've some left over that's gone stale, you now know what to do with it.

* *Source: Office of National Statistics*

FORGET THE SALT

Pane Toscano (Tuscan bread – opposite page, top) is oval in shape and rather bland as it's made without salt. There are two schools of thought as to why this is. The first is that it's often served with very salty ingredients, such as prosciutto or pecorino cheese, so salt in the bread isn't necessary. The second is that access to salt was at one time controlled by the seaport of Pisa, which taxed it. The Tuscans didn't want to pay, so made bread without it. The end product may have lacked taste, but at least it was cheap!

FASCINATING FACT

COOKED WATER

If the average Tuscan peasant didn't have the wherewithal for making soup, they made *acquacotta* (literally 'cooked water'). The ingredients were water, stale bread, onions and whatever else they could get their hands on.

FASCINATING FACT

BEAUTIFUL BREADCRUMBS

Any leftover bits of bread you have can be blitzed in a food processor to make breadcrumbs. These can then be used in everything from fishcakes to gratins and tarts. Alternatively, mixed with a little oil and parsley, they make a delicious crunchy topping on roast fish.

FASCINATING FACT

IS THIS BREAD FRESH?

A survey by the consumer group WRAP found that most consumers believed bread remained fresh for just three to four days. Yet in trials, it turned out that people couldn't tell the difference between bread that was two days old and bread that had been hanging around for six days.

FASCINATING FACT

BRING BACK THE BREAD BIN

The worst thing you can do to bread is keep it in the fridge, yet 9 per cent of people in the UK do exactly this. At a low temperature bread will actually go stale up to six times faster than in a bread bin.

MEET THE *BAKE OFF* TEAM

Behind the scenes there's a team of *Bake Off* heroes who bring the action in the tent to life. We meet some of the crew normally hidden from view and find out what goes on behind the cameras...

CHLOE AVERY
FOOD PRODUCER

What does your job involve?

We work closely with Mary and Paul and try to come up with new and interesting bakes. Once we've decided on them, I provide the bakers with a list of every Signature Bake and Showstopper they'll be expected to bake. The bakers have to outline every bake they will do before we start. Everybody who enters that tent in the first week has worked really hard before we've even filmed anything. We don't intervene. If two people are going to make the same thing, like when Kate and Chetna both made samosas, we just have to let that happen. It's quite interesting actually, because then you can compare the two bakes.

Are the bakers getting more and more ambitious with their recipes? You didn't get things like Nancy's choux windmill in the first year!

Yes. That's what is incredible about the show: it inspires people to be adventurous with their bakes. Every year the bakes seem to get more elaborate. What's great is that it inspires the viewers to be creative too.

Do the bakers provide you with a list of ingredients that they need?

Yes, and we check and double-check with them to make sure we have everything on the day. We also have someone on standby during the shoot to hop in a car to the supermarket, or they may actually be waiting at a supermarket just in case we need something!

What do you do while the bakes are going on?

I watch closely to see how the bakers are doing. I'm looking for amazing moments as well as mistakes, and feed that information back to the series producer and director. It's so important that we don't miss anything. So much of *Bake Off* is about the quiet moments, when they are biting their nails and watching the oven.

Don't you ever get sick, sampling all those cakes and biscuits?

I actually don't have much of a sweet tooth. After working on the show all day and being surrounded by cakes, the last thing I want is to eat them all, lovely and tasty though they are. But that's just me – the rest of the crew attack the bakes like gannets!

PAOLO PROTO
SERIES PRODUCER

What's the best thing about working on the show?

People get a lot out of it, more than just baking. They learn a lot about themselves. They learn about who they are and what they can achieve. It's about them overcoming obstacles and becoming the best they can be. One of the bakers emailed me and said, 'It's about a lot more than buns, Paolo.' That's so true.

Who does all the washing up?

The unsung heroes of *Bake Off*. There's a team of people dedicated to washing up after the bakers every weekend. When you think that often we've got stuff like hardened caramel in a pan, and they have 12 pans to wash, it's a big job. If the pans aren't washed, nobody can cook.

What does your job entail?

I manage all the different elements of the show: the food team, the editorial team, crew, everyone involved in making *Bake Off*. When filming is done, I also oversee the final edit. I have to have an overview of the entire production and of all the filming, which we then have to edit down to ten episodes.

Roughly how many hours of footage do you film for *Bake Off* every year?

Wow, lots! I would say for every week in the tent, we've filmed about 100 hours of footage.

What is the atmosphere like in that tent during filming?

First and foremost, the bakers are having a once-in-a-lifetime experience. We want that to be special for them and we want them to have fun and enjoy themselves, so we make a big effort to keep them happy. Mel and Sue, Mary and Paul and all the production team are really great people. On a sunny day, filming in a tent, you think, 'This is fantastic!'

ANDY DEVONSHIRE
SERIES DIRECTOR

What does your job involve?

I am responsible for filming inside the tent and out. I am a bit like the conductor of the *Bake Off* big band. I sit at the back of the tent with monitors showing all of the filming that's taking place. We don't want to miss anything, and every shot on *Bake Off* should tell a story.

Is it difficult keeping an eye on 12 different bakers at once?

The production team are on talkback, which means they're on headsets talking to each other all the time. There are producers on the floor feeding back to me and the series producer what is going on so that we capture the right stuff. They will flag, for example, when the cakes are going in or coming out of the oven, or if a baker is using a different technique from everyone else.

Do the cameras ever get in the way of the bakers?

I like to think of *Bake Off* as a bit like a wildlife show: we're trying to observe and not obstruct. We can never delay a baker just to get a particular shot. There are obviously some challenges, such as when it's very hot in the tent and they've made a fragile bake and it has to wait while we do what we call 'the beauty shot' before it gets seen by the judges. That's the shot of the finished bake looking beautiful.

Speaking of wildlife, are you responsible for the infamous squirrel shot in 2011?

I didn't film it, no! Every year I give a bottle of champagne to whoever captures the best shot of the series. Rick, our cameraman, captured that one. We did not predict how much attention that squirrel would get!

How has making the show changed since the first year?

I have a big affection for the very first cast, Edd's year. We all went in together not knowing how the show would work out. In the early days we travelled around the UK, which sounded like a great idea, but you didn't actually see much outside the tent. For Bread Week we pitched up next to a windmill in Kent, which is great because that's where bread-making begins. But windmills are obviously found in windy places, so it wasn't much fun for the sound guys having blasts of it whistling through the tent.

Bake Off secret!

The opening sequence of *Bake Off*, filmed back in 2010, was filmed in Andy's own house. 'We didn't have much money, so we just used my family kitchen,' he reveals. 'We did a slightly messier version of the pristine main credits for *An Extra Slice...*, for which my wife made the cakes. I'm quite proud of that fact when I see it on screen.'

JAKE SENIOR
MARY AND PAUL'S PRODUCER

What does your job involve?

A lot of my job is communicating to Paul and Mary what the bakers are making for the Signature Bake and Showstopper. I also oversee all the interviews they do to camera, and their little chats in their own tent. During their interviews, I might ask them to explain certain things about baking. They are both so knowledgeable that they might assume we viewers understand something we have no clue about, so I'll ask them to go into more detail.

Do you think the bakers are nervous of Mary and Paul?

Yes! The first time they meet them they are like rabbits caught in headlights. You can see the bakers almost stand to attention as they approach the bench. At that point I might have briefed Mary and Paul on what each baker is doing, and if there's anything interesting they might want to watch out for – perhaps an unusual ingredient, or a new technique.

Do the 'real' Mary and Paul come across on screen?

There's not much time in the show to get across their sense of humour. They are both very cheeky and quite often take the mickey out of each other, but they also clearly adore each other too.

What happens when they come to make their decision about who goes?

They will go off and discuss it alone. There is never any input from production at that point; it's purely down to Mary and Paul. It has to be just their decision.

Nancy from 2014 had a particularly sparkly rapport with Paul, didn't she?

Yes. What I loved about Nancy was that she wasn't fazed by anything at all. She just got on with it. We loved it when she called Paul 'the male judge'.

Have you personally ever been at the mercy of a 'Mary Berry death stare'?

Ha! Maybe. Mary is good at letting you know what she thinks with a look. But she's Mary Berry, she's earned that right!

Do you have a personal favourite bake from the show?

As crew, we never show favouritism with the bakes – we have to eat them all regardless!

MANDY READ
FLOOR MANAGER

What does your job involve?

I am basically the director's ears and eyes on the floor. I have to make sure the bakers are ready for the start of filming, make sure they are all in the right place. Once the baking has started, I make sure people can move about easily and I keep control of the tent. The floor of the tent is really bouncy, so I have to make sure people move carefully so as not to make the cameras bounce, and ensure nobody makes any noise. I'll call silence around the tent too so that filming can begin.

What about the mess in the tent – do you keep an eye on that?

Yes. The bakers on the whole are quite tidy, and we have runners who come in and take away tins and bowls they don't need any more. Every year, though, there will be one baker who's 'The Messy One'. Last year it was Richard: he was always spreading out his notes and his equipment and his ingredients, quite often all over the floor. I have to be careful of safety too. If I spot pan handles sticking out where cameramen need to walk, I'll have to go and make sure they are turned in the right way.

Do the bakers get to pick where they bake?

No, they are given a bench each week. Some of them don't like using the very front bench as they feel more exposed there. Martha last year hated being on the back bench – she thought it was unlucky.

How do you keep Mel and Sue under control?

I love Mel and Sue, they are so lovely. They will not stop talking, though! To the bakers, to the crew, to each other, they chat away. I do often have to gently remind them to move along to the next baker, or say it's time to leave the tent now. But they are great fun to work with.

FAENIA MOORE
HOME ECONOMIST

What does your job involve?

I am in charge of going through all the bakers' recipes and sourcing all the ingredients. On the day, I get the ingredients camera-ready, looking pretty and in their jars. I also do a formal briefing to the bakers about how to use all the equipment. For instance, they will be unfamiliar with the ovens we use, so we make sure they know how to use them properly.

Have you ever had a hard time sourcing an unusual ingredient?

Yes. Some of the bakers will get very specific about types of pastes or spices they need. Glenn from 2013 came up with some unusual challenges. We had to find isomalt for him, which is a kind of sweetener. In 2012 Brendan requested pärlsocker, which is a special variety of sugar. We could not find it anywhere, so in the end we had to track it down on the Internet and order it specially. Of course, a few months after it had been on TV, you could buy pärlsocker everywhere. The same thing happened with freeze-dried raspberries. We had to resort to picking them out of boxes of breakfast cereal, but since they were used on the show, you can probably get them in your corner shop.

What about Frances in 2013 – she used lots of ingredients, didn't she?

She would go a bit mad with her recipes. I remember once my colleague Georgia was working through one of her lists of ingredients and said, 'I'm on ingredient number 76, and I think I'm only halfway through!'

Do bakers bring in their own ingredients and lucky utensils?

Chetna in 2014 was very good at bringing in her own spices. Some of her chutneys were just gorgeous. I remember Mel encouraging her to start her own brand called 'Chetney'. One thing we discourage, though, is people bringing in anything sentimental. We had a baker back in the early days who brought in her great-grandmother's teaspoon for good luck. It inevitably got lost on the set. We did find it in the end, but from then on we really begged bakers not to bring anything like that on to the set.

Is it true you cook for Mary and Paul during filming?

Yes, me and my team are a little like a café for them! It doesn't really faze me making stuff for them any more, but Paul sometimes puts his judging hat on with me. I have to say to him, 'Do not dare try and critique that fry-up I have just made for you!' Mary's far more discreet.

ANNA BEATTIE
EXECUTIVE PRODUCER

What does your job involve?

I lead the *Bake Off* team and oversee the process from start to finish – from baker selection and choosing the challenges (which kicks off in the autumn) through filming in the spring/summer and then the edit. It's a year-round job, but it is such a brilliant team, who all do such a fab job, that I don't do much except encourage everybody these days!

How did *Bake Off* come about in the first place?

As a company, we have always been interested in how to take something that really happens and make it work for television – and we were convinced there was something in the village fête baking competition.

Was it difficult to persuade a channel to commission it?

Yes! It took us four years to convince someone that it was a good idea. And that someone was the brilliant woman running BBC2 at the time – Janice Hadlow. Still everybody said it couldn't be done because no one had ever tried before to make what would conventionally be a studio show in a tent. But we were adamant that it had to be outside. The tent caused all sorts of technical issues, but our amazing sound team and crew overcame them all. Only a real downpour gives us a problem now.

Has *Bake Off* changed?

Not much. The biggest change was between Series One and Series Two: we stopped moving the whole tent around the country, and we introduced the little Mary and Paul tent section, which I think really added to it.

Did you think it would be such a success?

No! We never imagined any of it. When we saw the first series in the edit, we knew it was good, but none of us ever imagined it would be what it is today. For so many people to love something we have all made is amazing.

Do you bake?

Yes – but my kids bake more!

CROSSWORD

Have a go at this puzzle – part general knowledge, part cryptic.

▼▼▼▼▼▼▼▼▼▼▼▼▼▼▼

ACROSS

1 Rolls popular in the northwest (4)

4 Snub backward bakes (4)

6, 12 Dessert made with puff pastry and caramelised fruit (5, 5)

8 Good bakes for a rainy day? (4,11)

9 Used for cooking and keeping cakes (4)

10 Batman and Robin, Simon and Garfunkel, Mel and Sue, for example (4)

15 Kitchen aid (6)

17 Cake, loaf, etc. that's well cooked throughout (4, 4)

18 Italian bread seasoned with olive oil and herbs (8)

19 Home of Romeo and Juliet and the sweet yeast bread pandoro (6)

21, 23, 24 Bake that's popular in heaven? (5, 4, 4)

25 This will tell you when you can start baking (4, 11)

26 Old-style cooker heated with wood or coal (5)

27 Type of whisk (4)

28 Quick bread, popular in Scotland and Ireland (4)

DOWN

2 Where 21, 23, 24 across was invented (7)

3 Prepares flour with mangled fists (5)

4 Grissino (10)

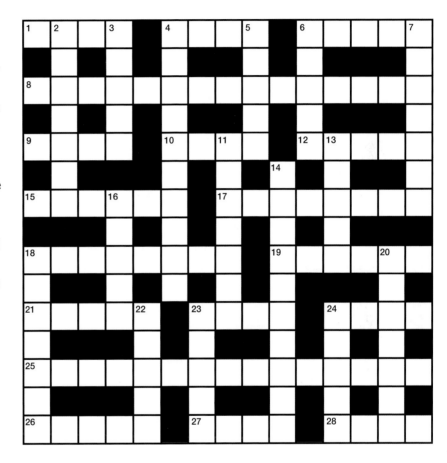

5 Parts of a potato, sometimes baked and filled (5)

6 Close, as in the texture of a bagel, or a Bake Off Final! (5)

7 Concentrated extract used to add flavour (7)

11 Aromatic herb often used on pizzas (7)

13 The colour of caramel when it's done (5)

14 A pork pie is a dish best _____ ____ (6, 4)

16 Coating applied to cakes, pies, etc. (5)

18 Bakes need lots of this to impress Paul and Mary (7)

20 Less strenuous method of making bread (2-5)

22 Thirty-five fluid ounces (5)

23 Not stale (5)

24 They're paid to cook (5)

▼▼▼▼▼▼▼▼▼▼▼▼▼▼▼▼▼▼▼▼▼▼▼

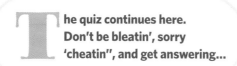

The quiz continues here. Don't be bleatin', sorry 'cheatin'', and get answering...

THE GREAT BIG *BAKE OFF* QUIZ
ROUND THREE

▼ ▼ ▼ ▼ ▼ ▼ ▼ ▼ ▼ ▼ ▼ ▼ ▼ ▼

1. What is Norman teaching Sue in this classic moment from 2014?

a. Dance robotics
b. Boxing skills
c. How to spell 'bake' in semaphore
d. Falconry

2. Mary wasn't happy with one element of Brendan's Gingerbread Bird House in 2012's Biscuit Week. What was it?

a. The roof – which he'd built with shop-bought breakfast cereal
b. The bird – which he'd not made edible
c. The walls – which weren't smoothly connected to one another
d. The icing – which wasn't piped on neatly

3. What did Sue do to Howard's English Muffins in 2013?

a. Accidentally leant on them with her elbow
b. Mistakenly ate one, thinking it was going spare
c. Knocked them off his worktop
d. Juggled with them

4. In 2012 Cathryn served up Lady Arundel's Manchet as a Signature Bake. What the heck is a manchet?

a. A type of sweet bread
b. An upside-down pudding
c. A steamed cake
d. A meat pie

5. Mary liked the Hidden Carrot Cake produced by Frances in 2013, but what did she say was the one thing that could have been done to improve it?

a. Hidden a real carrot in it
b. Toned down the colours
c. Made edible plant pots rather than using real ones
d. Made it bigger

6. In 2012, which London landmark did Danny create in Biscuit Week?

a. Big Ben
b. The London Eye
c. Buckingham Palace
d. St Paul's Cathedral

7-11. Can you identify these four bakers from their features?

12. In 2013 Glenn and Robert both baked a Spanakopita. Where does this pie originate?

a. Spain
b. Germany
c. Greece
d. Israel

13. What kind of pastry is a Spanakopita traditionally made with?

a. Shortcrust
b. Filo
c. Choux
d. Hot-water crust

14. Nancy's 2014 final Showstopper was a reproduction of what structure?

a. A Dutch windmill
b. Blackpool Tower
c. The Moulin Rouge
d. *The Great British Bake Off* tent

15. And in the same challenge, who presented the bake below?

a. Luis b. Martha
c. Richard d. Norman

16. What animal did Brendan shape choux pastries to resemble in 2012's Patisserie Challenge? (The answer is somewhere in this book.)

a. Peacocks b. Squirrels
c. Hedgehogs d. Swans

17. What cardinal sin did Enwezor commit when making his Biscuit Rocket Showstopper in 2014?

a. He presented burnt biscuits.
b. He used too much shop-bought fondant.
c. The rocket failed to stand up.
d. He failed to finish it.

18. Can you name this baker from 2010 hidden behind the pear?

a. David b. Mark
c. Edd d. Jonathan

19. 'I'm not terribly fond of chocolate,' Howard claimed in 2013. Why is he not a fan?

a. It makes him sleepy.
b. It gives him a migraine.
c. It gives him funny dreams.
d. He ate a dodgy Wagon Wheel in the 1980s and hasn't forgotten it.

20. Which baker has been crowned Star Baker five times – more than any other baker in the tent's history?

a. Holly b. Richard
c. James d. Ruby

21. Which baker dropped their Chocolate Fondants on the floor in 2012's Pudding Week?

a. John b. Cathryn
c. Brendan d. Danny

22. Who was named *The Great British Bake Off* winner in 2011?

a. Holly b. Jasminder
c. Mary-Anne d. Jo

Can you identify the following three bakers from their clothes?

23. He was the boy from the Shetlands, but even in the stifling heat, he wouldn't surrender his beloved woollen tank top.

a. Norman b. James
c. Ben d. Jason

24. She might've been a traditional baker, but she rocked the sporty footwear in the tent.

a. Mary-Anne b. Chetna
c. Diana d. Yasmin

25. This self-confessed baking geek loved his printed shirts.

a. Robert b. Luis
c. Jordan d. Edward

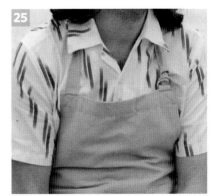

The quiz continues on page 108
The answers are on page 124

From Custard to Mustard: consider the condiments

Whatever you're baking in the kitchen, spare a thought for the condiments. Far from being mere sidekicks, they are the unsung heroes that help lift your efforts from good to great. For savoury bakes, you need a punchy condiment, and they don't come punchier than English mustard – perfect on a ham sandwich made with homemade bread, or with a slice of pork pie.

ONE OF THE first commercial mustard powders was made by a Mrs Clements of Durham in 1720. She ground mustard seeds to a fine powder using a mill rather than a pestle and mortar as chefs had done for centuries. This produced a stronger mustard with much more flavour, which people loved. Some producers later emulated the process, particularly Colman's of Norwich, who added turmeric to produce the distinctive bright yellow colour we enjoy today.

For sweet bakes, such as fruit pies and crumbles, the condiment has got to be custard, one of the few creations the French actually attribute to us by name: crème anglaise. It can even be the main event in dishes such as custard tarts or Trinity Burnt Cream. A proper custard should be light, delicate and creamy, rather than the neon yellow 'gloop' you probably got at school.

For those who didn't have access to fresh eggs to make a custard from scratch, custard powder was the next best thing. It was invented by Victorian chemist Alfred Bird because his wife was allergic to eggs. He combined cornflour with annatto colouring, derived from a South American nut, that turned it yellow. You simply added sugar and hot milk to the powder and stirred until thick. It was cheap, never curdled and could be poured on everything.

And what about ice cream, which is not only a side accompaniment, but also a main event in dishes such as Arctic roll and baked Alaska? Everyone's heard of Mrs Beeton, but hardly anyone's heard of Agnes Marshall, who was hailed in her time as the 'Queen of Ices' for her pioneering work on ice cream. She published four cookery books and ran a cookery school in Mortimer Street, London. The Victorians for whom Marshall was catering loved ice creams, sorbets and other frozen dishes, and even made them from ingredients we would find unusual today, such as cucumber and asparagus. However, Agnes Marshall's biggest contribution to baking is popularising the ice cream cone. This biscuity container replaced the unhygienic glass dishes known as 'penny licks', which were popular with ice cream vendors.

So consider your condiments: if you're serving crumble without custard, or a pork pie without mustard, a vital ingredient is missing.

FASCINATING FACT

ASIAN CUSTARDS

Many Asian cuisines don't include dairy products, but a few nonetheless have dishes that are similar to set custards. These tend to be savoury. For example, *chawanmushi* (literally 'teacup steam') combines beaten eggs with a fish-based stock, mushrooms or seafood. Sounds unusual, but many medieval set-custard dishes featured savoury additions, such as pounded pork and sage as well.

The custard that's been 'burnt' for over 400 years

'Burnt custard', perhaps best known by its French name *crème brûlée*, has not changed much in over 400 years. The recipe in T. Williams' 1717 book *The Accomplished Housekeeper and Universal Cook* recommends adding a little lemon peel and a spoonful of orange flower water to the custard mixture. It then adds, 'When it is cold, sift a quarter of a pound of sugar all over it, and brown it with a hot salamander [a piece of metal heated in the fire] till it looks like a glass plate put over your cream.'

FASCINATING FACT

FISHY KETCHUP

The word 'ketchup' comes from the Chinese *kêtsiap*, which means 'fish-based sauce'. Merchants brought both the sauce and the word back to Europe, where it was later applied to table sauces made from other ingredients, such as mushrooms, oysters or walnuts. By the 1800s, tomato ketchup recipes began to appear in America and Europe, and in 1869 H.J. Heinz starting producing his version of tomato ketchup, which was to become iconic.

FRANCES

The arrival of Frances on the *Bake Off* scene changed everything. No longer was a cake just a teatime treat – it was also an artistic extravaganza. In Frances' mind, if a biscuit didn't come with a theme and a back-story, it wasn't worth dunking in your tea. The road to victory saw the children's clothing designer having to defend her creativity to the hilt, and prove that art and baking do go hand in hand. Frances looks back over her time in the tent...

2013

CAKE WEEK

Start as you mean to go on

Frances burst into action in the tent with the first Signature Bake, a sandwich cake. Showing that she was no run-of-the-mill baker, her Giant Jam Sandwich Cake was shaped into an actual sandwich, complete with icing paper bag!

Story of the squirrel

It was when Frances crafted her 'Secret Squirrel' Showstopper cake, complete with a hidden squirrel centre, that we really sat up and took notice.

'Everybody thought I was doing the squirrel because of the *Bake Off* squirrel [see page 86], but actually it was a cake I had baked before, for someone I worked with whose nickname was "Squirrel". She was pregnant and we were calling the baby the "secret squirrel". It was quite a personal bake for me.'

Paul felt the cake was a little dense inside, but it was a strong start for Frances, for whom hiding a woodland creature in a cake was just the beginning.

BREAD WEEK

On fire

Frances' Signature Bake – Chilli, Chocolate and Ginger Matchstick Breadsticks – is one of the most memorable bakes to feature on the show, with a specially built oversized matchbox to display them.

'I'm a *Blue Peter* child; I've always been creative. I'm really proud of that bake. I used to hear people in the street whisper, "That's the matches girl," after that show went out.'

It wasn't all good news. Although both judges loved the box, Paul warned that the dough needed more work.

PIES AND TARTS WEEK

Style over substance

Frances' Peach Pie in the Sky Signature Bake heralded the start of her biggest challenge in the tent. Not impressed with the taste, Paul told the disappointed baker, 'I love your style, but please remember the substance.'

'I remember going home and saying to my brother: "Paul said I was more style over substance." My brother said, "I wouldn't worry about it. I am sure they won't make anything of it." Little did we know how that phrase would take off!'

BISCUIT AND TRAYBAKE WEEK

Last-minute changes

So rattled was Frances by the words of the judges that she made a decision she would live to regret for the Biscuit Week Showstopper.

'I had intended to make a Gingerbread House of Cards with Mary [Berry] Queen of Hearts cards and Paul Hollywood jokers. But I was worried because it used just one type of gingerbread and I thought they'd say they wanted more substance. So I changed my plan to a haberdashery box theme. I chucked in every type of button – peanut butter, vanilla, marbled chocolate and cinnamon.'

The change didn't pay off when the biscuit tower collapsed, leaving Frances to face tough scrutiny from Mary and Paul.

PASTRY WEEK

High praise

It was during Pastry Week that Frances started to shine brightly, when her Showstopper, three types of puff pastry bakes, was a resounding hit. 'Good flavours... I'll go for that,' Mary beamed, tucking into Sheet Music Mille-feuille. Oh yes, of course they had a theme – pastry inspired by the music of Edith Piaf. Why not?

'It was incredible to win Star Baker, especially for puff pastry, which I'd never made, and I'm not in a rush to ever make again!'

FREE-FROM WEEK

In for the kill

Mary's praise didn't extend to Frances' next Showstopper, a Hidden Carrot Cake. Despite slaving away to produce a visually impressive potted plant scene, Frances had rattled the judge. 'You haven't made your pots,' she critiqued.

'I'd made the main pot with icing, and just used a couple of real ones for decoration. She wanted blood, did Mary! I'd made chocolate soil, edible plants... what more did they want!'

FINAL

The last big bake

With just Ruby and Kimberley left as her rivals to the crown, Frances really pushed the boat out with her final Showstopper, a *Midsummer Night's Dream* Wedding Cake.

'I think I broke all *Bake Off* records with the amount of ingredients I used. It was over 150! The thing was huge.'

WINNER!

Frances was announced the fourth *Bake Off* winner in a Final that left everybody guessing until the very last moment.

'By the end I just felt so physically and emotionally drained. When I heard my name my legs went wobbly. If Ruby hadn't been next to me, I probably would've collapsed. It was an amazing moment.'

SINCE *BAKE OFF*...

Bake Off taught her some big life lessons

'I have learned a lot about not giving up. There were maybe times before *Bake Off* where I'd be more inclined to throw in the towel. *Bake Off* taught me that it's worth persevering and taking criticism on the chin, but not letting it change who you are.'

It took her two years from winning to perfect her first cookbook

'I didn't want to just rush a recipe book out really quickly, one that I wasn't especially happy with. I wanted to find the time to do it properly. I'm not just doing the

recipes: I've done lots of the artwork, I've been involved in all the photo shoots. For me, having that creative input has been a brilliant process.'

Frances' other love is music

'One of the hardest things in the *Bake Off* tent was baking without music or having the radio on. I quite often time my bakes to *Desert Island Discs*, and I'm always inspired by music. Since the show I've baked for Jules Holland, Lionel Richie and Coldplay. I'm a huge Chris Martin fan. In fact "Viva la Vida" was the song I listened to on my way to the tent for the Final: it's like my anthem!'

She has plenty of ambitions to fulfil

'I'm quite sporty and I would love to run a marathon one day. I've also always had a passion for cinnamon, so I'd like to travel to Scandinavia and visit the bakeries where they make all the spiced pastries.'

YOUR BAKES FROM HOME

T he Showstopper of 2014's Final saw Nancy, Richard and Luis all make an edible re-creation of a place that was very special to them. Luis' tribute to his hometown of Poynton competed against Nancy's Moulin Rouge and Richard's Mill Hill windmill efforts. Your own baking is just as personal, as proven by these bakes based on favourite or iconic places.

Personal Bakes

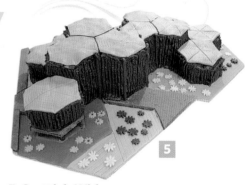

1. Allotment Cake
Made by Rebecca from Blackwood

Check out this very tidy allotment design. Baked for her father's birthday, Rebecca's cake has everything from mini carrots and cauliflowers to a leaking watering can!

2. Corfe Castle
Made by Dawn from Wiltshire

Dawn made this edible version of Corfe Castle for her father, to evoke memories of his birthplace. The detailing of the windows and roof slates is top notch.

3. Lazy Sunday
Made by Ruth from Leicester

Modelled on a personal favourite place – the sofa on a Sunday with the dog – this cake is packed with personality, right down to the scattered magazines and creased jeans. We think it's great.

4. London Town, Baby!
Made by Simon from Berkshire

How do you cram the whole of London onto a cake? Just ask Simon. This complicated design has it all: Big Ben, The Shard and even the London Eye are all featured. Impressive work, we say.

5. Scottish Widows
Made by Claire from Edinburgh

A cake tribute to one of Edinburgh's less-celebrated architectural designs – the Scottish Widows office! This cake was made as part of Edinburgh's annual Cake Fest. We hope you came out tops for your originality, Claire.

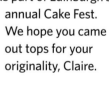

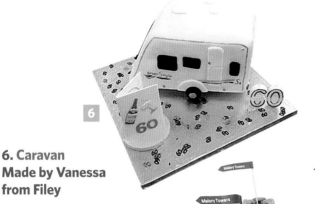

6. Caravan
Made by Vanessa from Filey

This fruit cake, decorated with marzipan and fondant icing, is a replica of Vanessa's favourite place – her caravan!

7. Downton Abbey
Made by Laura from Durham

A fan of the popular period drama, Laura has made a sponge scale model of *Downton Abbey*'s set, Highclere Castle. It's an impressive structure that Mrs Patmore herself would be proud to serve up!

8. Malory Towers
Made by Jen Dyke from Nottingham

Inspired by her favourite Enid Blyton books, Jen's made a cake version of the fictional boarding school Malory Towers. Super turret work, Jen! She even apologises for not making edible flags. We're sure Mary would forgive you!

9. Carlisle Old Town Hall
Made by Lisa from Carlisle

This cake takes every little detail of Carlisle's well-known town hall and translates it into icing. The individual tile work and the tricky staircase are so impressive, it would be a shame to cut into it!

10. L'Arc de Triomphe
Made by Helen from Newcastle upon Tyne

Ooh la la! This cake and fondant construction has Paris's Arc de Triomphe down to the very finest of details. Topiary trees lining the Champs-Élysées and little French policemen on motorbikes give it a very special *je ne sais quoi*!

11. My Best Friend's Garden
Made by Sandra from Chingford

Sandra designed and created this cake for her best friend's birthday. Using crafty icing design, she's managed to create her favourite place, her garden, and even modelled her pal on the bench enjoying it. We bet she loved this.

Can you journey deep into the treacle tart and find your way to the cherry in the centre?

LOST IN THE LATTICE

SPOT THE DIFFERENCE

Can you spot the 10 differences between these two images?

ANSWERS

1. Colour of Paul's shirt. 2. Tartan colour on flask. 3. Teacup colour. 4. The tent is gone. 5. A lamb has appeared. 6. The flask cup has been replaced by a cup of coffee. 7. A plane has appeared in the sky. 8. The straps have gone from the hamper. 9. The blueberries on the far left have been replaced with strawberries. 10. Paul's foot has gone from behind Mary's leg.

What got you into baking?

I've baked since I was a child. My family always baked.

Tell us about your earliest food memory.

Something called 'grey pastry', which was what I made from leftover pastry my mum had made. It was grey from hours of me messing with it, adding everything from Marmite to hundreds-and-thousands.

What's your guilty food pleasure?

Mashed potato! Mash with gravy, with cheese, even in a sandwich!

If you could invite anyone past or present around for tea, who would it be and what would you bake?

Al Pacino or Keith Richards, because with those faces they must have interesting stories to tell! I'd probably bake something with alcohol in, a really nice chocolate tart with amaretto, or really good biscotti with vin santo.

If you could bake only one thing, what would it be?

Cornish pasties. They're so comforting.

When you're not baking, how do you relax?

I like my real fire, a good film and a glass of red wine. Or I buy shoes. I'm on 98 pairs. I wear my new shoes when I'm baking as it helps break them in a bit.

Who do you like to bake for?

I like to bake for friends and family, and colleagues at school.

Tell us about running your school's cookery club.

It's for children with special challenges, and promotes baking and cooking on a budget. It's hard work when you've already done your day job, but so rewarding. One girl has since gone on to catering college, and now has an apprenticeship in a restaurant. The club lets the students see their successes quickly, and they can see the success in themselves.

What are your five favourite bakes?

Chicken and ham raised pie, ricciarelli [a soft almond macaron from northern Italy], chocolate tart or lemon tart, biscuits (because you get a lot for your efforts) and biscotti.

What's your worst baking disaster?

The worst disaster happened with the base of a wedding cake. I put it down to pick up the phone, then I was walking backwards – probably in painful shoes – and sat down on it. I had to start all over again.

What's the most surprising, unusual or interesting thing in your cupboard?

Liquorice root powder, which is a sludgy green colour. I got it for a biscuit recipe I'm working on. The biscuits have this subtle liquorice taste, but they look awful, so it may be back to the drawing board with that one.

What's your favourite kitchen gadget?

I like my mandoline and food processor, but generally I'm not really into gadgets. I think you can do a lot with just a small sharp knife.

Describe your kitchen at home.

My son built the cupboards, and they are open shelving, as I like things on show. I've a double-range gas cooker, and the sink was specially made in France.

What's your favourite ingredient to work with?

Pastry, because it is so versatile. You can make a meat pie, and with the leftovers make tarts for pudding. The possibilities are never-ending.

Do you keep a recipe notebook?

No. I have an empty recipe notebook, and every time I look at it I think I should use it, but I don't. I do have my ex-mother-in-law's, though.

What's your party trick?

I can sing a bit, things like old Irish songs.

Tell us one thing about yourself that will surprise us?

I'm a fully qualified hypnotherapist.

What did it feel like when you found out you'd been selected for *Bake Off* 2015?

It was surreal – like it was happening to someone else. In fact, I still have to pinch myself to make sure I'm not dreaming and that all this has really happened to me.

How did you prepare for *Bake Off*?

I practised, I doubted myself, and practised, and doubted some more, and practised again. I did some self-hypnosis and things to convince myself that somebody had seen something in me and I had to go and prove them right.

What's your favourite *Bake Off* moment from a previous series?

I enjoyed watching Norman. When everyone else was doing decoration, he just did icing sugar, loads of it.

Who's your favourite past baker and why?

Nancy, I really identify with her. She did things because it's what you do with families in mind. It wasn't baking for competition, it's baking because it's what you do. I bake because I enjoy it and people like it. I bake with my heart, not my head, and felt as though Nancy did the same thing.

What got you into baking?

It was thanks to home economic lessons at school. I particularly liked bread dough and the chemistry side of things. I was fascinated by how yeast works, and of course, the delicious results sealed the deal.

Tell us about your earliest food memory.

I grew up on a farm in Devon, but one of my earliest memories is of being blown away by the food on a family holiday to Orlando, Florida, when I was seven. There were things like pancakes and maple syrup, and vast buffets of shellfish and lobsters, things I just hadn't seen before.

What's your guilty food pleasure?

Sweet and sour chicken – the sort in luminous orange sauce.

If you could invite anyone past or present around for tea, who would it be and what would you bake?

It would have to be my late dad. He knew how important music was to me, but didn't get to see how food would become such a big part of my life. I'd make us both a Beef Wellington.

If you could bake only one thing, what would it be?

It would have to be bread.

When you're not baking, how do you relax?

I like making and listening to music, as well as hanging out with my family.

Do you listen to music when you're baking?

Yes, I do. Calm sounds if I'm making something intricate, but heavier stuff, like heavy metal or drum and bass, if I'm kneading dough.

If you only had time for one thing, would it be baking or music?

Well, baking is currently taking over from the music, but they're both so important that I couldn't imagine not having either in my life.

Who do you like to bake for?

I like baking for my friends. People always receive sweet carb-based things with a positive reaction.

What are your five favourite bakes?

I'm a big fan of a custard slice, and I love French patisserie, so something like pain aux raisins. I'd also go for pork pie, hot fresh cinnamon rolls and pizza.

What's your worst baking disaster?

I've had issues in the past with hot hands on warm days, and 'pastry rage' has happened on more than one occasion. My wife can attest to me screaming into a tea towel.

What's the most surprising, unusual or interesting thing in your cupboard?

A massive tub of foaming sourdough starter. Unless they're keen bakers, most people don't have that in their cupboard.

What's your favourite kitchen gadget?

I love my blowtorch. It does something for my inner delinquent!

What's your favourite ingredient to work with?

I find eggs fascinating. They can be runny, foamy, set hard, help cakes to rise – they're incredible.

Do you keep a recipe notebook?

I do, and a blog because my handwriting's awful. I like to keep a record of my experiments.

What's your party trick?

It's fairly limited to providing good food.

Tell us one thing about yourself that will surprise us.

I once had a Saturday job in Woking as a shopping centre mascot called Snappy the Alligator. I had to strip down to my underwear and put on this massive polystyrene costume that made me sweat constantly. Sometimes my handler would wander off and I'd be left roaming around, not really able to see anything and unnerving shoppers.

What did it feel like when you found out you'd been selected for *Bake Off* 2015?

Well, I applied as a bit of a punt. In the past, lack of time has stopped me from applying, but I had a break in my touring schedule and wasn't going to be away for a long

time, so I took a chance. When I got the call after the long audition process, I was elated. I've always had a love of food and this gave me the opportunity to put some energy into it.

How did you prepare for *Bake Off*?

I just figured I'd try to cook stuff I thought they'd like. Nothing too fancy, but things that taste good. I tried to come up with new flavour combinations, as well as turning out a few various classics.

What's your favourite *Bake Off* moment from previous series?

What I like most when watching the show is the feeling of the bakers being like a family. It's a close-knit group, and there's a genuine sadness when someone has to go. The warmth of the show comes through in those moments.

Who's your favourite past baker and why?

John Whaite. I think he's got some good ideas and knows what he's talking about. I was rooting for him and made a mini victory lap of the lounge when he won!

Who could have imagined that Dessert Week in 2013 would lead to events that would shake the tent to its very foundations (well, groundsheet). The apparently simple task of making a trifle left a shameful trail of custard and chaos never before seen in *Bake Off* history. Behold the story of how Deborah and Howard's custard got mixed up in *Bake Off*'s great 'crime anglaise'!

CUSTARD-GATE!

On your marks, get set, **bake!**

As the Signature Challenge began, who knew what trifle-based carnage lay ahead?

Not Howard, happily tinkering away at his Caramel and Apple recipe...

Nor Deborah, whose Tropical Trifle was about to cause a tropical storm...

Your custard looks nice...

Not as yummy as yours does!

You're making a true crème anglaise? You're the bravest baker in the tent.

It was all going so swimmingly...

I've impressed Mary – what could possibly go wrong?

I'll just pop my custard in to cool, next to Deborah's identical glass bowl...

"Once this layer's done, I'll add my custard..."

But Deborah was about to make a terrible mistake...

"Hang on...this custard doesn't look like mine. OH, CRIPES!"

Where's my custard?

"Right, Howard. The thing is..."

It was confession time for unwitting baking bandit Deborah.

"I'm sure one's as good as another."

"Even if I did make a tricky crème anglaise and she bunged some cornflour in..."

Howard seemed to take the custard swap in good humour...

Just for a moment, Howard considered giving Deborah a custard shampoo...

Meanwhile, Deborah was so full of regret that she couldn't even look at the scene of the crime.

"So long as there's sherry in this trifle, I don't care where the custard came from!"

When it came to judging, things were a trifle confusing for Paul and Mary.

"I nearly started another Cold War."

Did Deborah have any regrets about the trifle fiasco? Yes – hundreds and thousands.

The bakers gathered to hear their fate...

"Can somebody book me a cab home? My knees have turned to jelly."

"It's not mine, is it?"

It was goodbye to Deborah, who left the tent with a feeling of genuine remorse – as well as Sue's glasses, Paul's hair gel and one of Mary's floral jackets (allegedly).

THE GREAT BIG *BAKE OFF* QUIZ
ROUND FOUR

▼ ▼ ▼ ▼ ▼ ▼ ▼ ▼ ▼ ▼ ▼ ▼ ▼ ▼

1. In 2014, why did Chetna have a slight advantage when baking her Povitica Technical Challenge?

a. She makes it every week for her family.
b. She makes them for a living.
c. She had already made it for her Signature Bake.
d. She invented the Povitica nut roll.

2. What did Lucy, Christine, Ruby and Howard all manage to do in the first episode of 2013?

a. Cut themselves
b. Drop their bakes
c. Forget an ingredient
d. Forget to preheat their ovens

3. What name did 2014's Jordan give to his 'pet' yeast? (The answer can be found in this book.)

a. Yorick
b. Paul
c. Beasty
d. Mr Magoo

4. What was unusual about the 2012 Final, in which John was the winner?

a. It was the first all-male Final.
b. It was broadcast live.
c. None of the bakers had previously been crowned Star Baker.
d. The bakers wore fancy dress.

5. Peter in 2012 had a framed photo of who on his bench in the tent?

a. His family   b. Mary Berry
c. The Queen   d. Mel and Sue

6–10. Can you name these tricky Technical bakes?

a. Dacquoise   b. Florentines
c. Rum Baba   d. Chocolate Roulade
e. Chocolate Teacakes

11. In 2014, what did Nancy controversially do while baking her Lincolnshire Plum Loaf? (Search this book for the answer.)

a. Put it in the fridge.
b. Didn't leave it to prove it at all.
c. Steamed it to help it rise.
d. Used the microwave to prove it.

12. What unusual ingredient did Howard use in his Sweet Tea Loaf in 2013?

a. Popcorn b. Aloe vera
c. Charcoal d. Hemp

13. And what reaction did that earn from Mary?

a. She told him not to use it.
b. She asked for his recipe.
c. She said she knew nothing about it.
d. She laughed hysterically.

14. Who was the first-ever person to be crowned Star Baker?

a. Holly b. Janet
c. Mary-Anne d. Yasmin

15. What kitchen item did Ruby manage to break during her time in the tent in 2013?

a. Her oven
b. A whisk
c. A mixing bowl
d. The fridge door

16. Which baker is Sue offering support to below in 2013, after her crème patissière curdled?

a. Frances b. Ruby
c. Kimberley d. Christine

17. What was the theme of Frances' Showstopper Wedding Cake in 2013?

a. Cupid
b. *Romeo and Juliet*
c. Bridal dress
d. *A Midsummer Night's Dream*

18. Complete this Paul Hollywood quote: 'Understand ____, understand baking.'

a. Flour
b. Bread
c. Mary
d. Me

19. Which of the following bakers did not make it to the Final in 2014?

a. Richard b. Chetna
c. Luis d. Nancy

20. How did Paul describe John's Chocolate Torte in 2012?

a. A chocolate catastrophe
b. A chocolate breezeblock
c. A giant doorstop
d. A plank of wood

21–25. (right) Can you match the names of these bakers to their photos?

a. Toby
b. Mark
c. Annetha
d. Cathryn
e. Victoria

The answers are on page 124

NANCY

With her straight-talking, no-nonsense approach to baking, Nancy impressed judges and viewers alike right from the off. The Hull-born grandmother brought years of experience into the tent, and with her professional-looking bakes and maverick use of the microwave, she left as the winner, forgetting any plans she might have had for a quiet retirement. Nancy tells us about her time on *Bake Off*, and what she's up to now...

2014

CAKE WEEK

A star is born!

Nancy started as she meant to go on when she was named the first Star Baker of 2014. Her first Signature Bake – a Coffee and Hazelnut Swiss roll – impressed both Mary and Paul, but it was the Technical Challenge – a Cherry Cake – that had Mary enraptured. 'Perfect nuts,' she commented, later declaring Nancy's cake the best of the bunch.

'Hearing that I was Star Baker was brilliant. I remember looking around the tent while we were baking on that first day. Everybody was decorating their Swiss rolls apart from me. I left mine quite simple, and I thought to myself, "Maybe I shouldn't be here." Everybody was so talented. So to be made Star Baker gave me comfort that I did deserve my place in the tent.'

DESSERT WEEK

Ice scream

A Baked Alaska Showstopper had all the bakers hot under the collar – not least because they were making an ice cream dish on a roasting hot day. But Nancy breezed through with her own summer fruit version, which Paul described as 'exceptional'.

'I was probably the only one whose ice cream didn't melt. I'd figured out that we didn't have very long for it to set, so I always planned to make three small blocks of ice cream rather than a single big one, and it worked. I think that was probably one of the hardest challenges. I've certainly not made a Baked Alaska since!'

PIES AND TARTS WEEK

Dangerous

When Nancy showed Paul and Mary the depth of the tin for her Signature Bake – a Chocolate-crusted Passion Fruit Tart – Paul worried that it was far too shallow. Labelling the choice 'dangerous', it was one of many times that he expressed concerns about Nancy's baking 'risks'.

'At the start he would put the fear of God into me, but I turned it into a bit of fun. I'd say, "Oh, here he comes, what now?" That's why I'd start joking and call him "The Male Judge". I never used to let him get to me. He's a real softie, actually. He was wrong about that pie tin, anyway!'

He certainly was, having to eat his words along with her tart, and admit it tasted 'very, very good'.

EUROPEAN CAKE WEEK

Baking into the unknown

Although Nancy came first in the Swedish Princess Cake Technical Challenge, it was a bake she had never heard of.

'I don't think there was a single Technical Challenge that I was familiar with making, and I'd never heard of a few of them! I'd never seen a Swedish Princess Cake before, but it saved my bacon a bit because my Signature Bake – a Rum Punch Savarin – was awful.'

ADVANCED DOUGH WEEK

Baking a judge

As well as winding up Paul by controversially proving her Signature Bake, a Lincolnshire Plum Loaf, in the microwave, Nancy took their playful sparring one step further when she recreated Paul's face on one of her Chocolate and Orange Doughnuts for the Showstopper round!

'When I was doing the funny faces on the doughnuts, I made the eyes blue. I thought, "Oh, if I add grey hair, these would look like Paul." It was Sue's idea to do one with a miserable face! He didn't crack a smile at all – maybe it was a bit cheeky!'

The judging table didn't raise big smiles for Nancy either, with Paul deeming her doughnuts 'slightly overdone'.

SEMI-FINAL PATISSERIE WEEK
Final countdown

As the Final came within reach, the bakers faced tough scrutiny in the Technical Challenge. Paul demanded a 20-layer Schichttorte, but Nancy, having only enough mixture for 18 layers, shrugged and said: 'Oh well, who's counting?' Paul – that's who! – much to the horror of Nancy and Chetna, who also fell below the layer count for this grilled cake.

'As soon as he started counting, I knew I was in trouble! I think the Semi-final was the most challenging week. By this point we were all so exhausted. I think I only got through because my Baklava Signature Bakes were good.'

THE FINAL
One last bake

Having made it to the Final along with Richard and Luis, Nancy's last Showstopper was a Pièce Montée – a real chance to demonstrate what she could do. Her choux, caramel and shortbread structure inspired by the windmill atop the Moulin Rouge in Paris was an elaborate creation that pushed her to the limits.

'I was up at 4.30am on the day of the Final practising it!'

It was a hit. 'You should be very proud of that,' Mary said of the bake's appearance, before both judges gave it a positive reaction on taste too.

WINNER!

After ten long weeks, Nancy was finally crowned the winner!

'I honestly don't remember much at all after the moment they said my name. It was a real blur. I felt a huge sense of relief and sadness at the same time that it was over.'

SINCE *BAKE OFF*...

Having worked for the NHS as a GP practice manager for nearly 30 years, *Bake Off* gave recently retired Nancy a new career:

'I couldn't wait to retire, but I found that I missed the routine of work. *Bake Off* brought me out of retirement and I couldn't be more grateful. Now I'm so busy and I'm doing things I am really passionate about.'

She's become a judge in her own right

'I've done a lot of judging at village shows and baking competitions. *Bake Off* has given me the confidence to give people feedback on where they've gone wrong, or what they can do to improve something. I feel I can talk with authority now.'

She's baked for the cast of *EastEnders*

'They asked me to bake a cake for the soap's thirtieth anniversary, so I made a cake of Albert Square and the Queen Vic. I delivered it to the set and I got a kiss from Danny Dyer. It was great! Moments like that I do catch myself thinking, "How on earth did I get here?"'

Whether you're fiddling with filo, tackling a Technical or being flamboyant with your flavours, as a baker in the tent, you should have only one ultimate aim. And that's to impress those very exacting food judges, Mary and Paul. In the six years of *Bake Off*, they have forensically analysed and critically appraised 161 challenges – over 1400 different bakes. As well as having an encyclopedic knowledge of their specialism, our gimlet-eyed pair know a thing or two about endurance, particularly as more than a few of the bakes have suffered from an excess of moisture in the bottom department.

Here we offer some hints or tips for impressing them...

A simple (but in no way foolproof) guide to

TRYING TO IMPRESS MARY AND PAUL

 Try ingratiating yourself by choosing ingredients you know they like.

It's an open secret that Paul and Mary have their favourite flavours.

Mary, for example, is known not to be a fan of anything too spicy, a fact Kate took into account during Pastry Week when making her Spinach and Paneer Samosa. She told Mary she'd reduced the fire of the spices just for her, to which Paul shrugged, 'I like things spicy.' In the end, she gained nothing in trying to please because while she fussed over her spices, she lost sight of the fact her pastry wasn't cooked properly!

DON'T! **Choose ingredients you know they hate.**

Basically, avoid the use of lavender in meringue.

End of.

 Listen carefully. If they describe your baking as 'courageous' or 'daring', immediately stop whatever you're doing.

Martha's 2014 Bread Week provides a good example. Happily kneading her date and walnut rye dough, which included treacle for added depth of colour, Paul was intrigued to find she was planning on using an egg wash before baking it. 'That's very daring,' he opined, his troubled expression seeming to challenge Martha into trying to figure out just why. 'I won't tell you why... I'll talk about it later,' he said, and cheerfully left Martha with a terrible sense of dread. Lo and behold, when Martha produced the rolls for judging, Paul unlocked the mystery. Putting the egg glaze on top, he said, had 'falsely accused' the rolls

of being ready, so Martha had taken the bread out too early.

Future bakers take note: hone your mind-reading skills before going into the tent, as crystal balls are not supplied by the *Bake Off* team.

DON'T! Present them with an invisible bake.

Iain's Baked Alaska back in 2014's Dessert Week may have been a melting mess of ice cream and meringue, but his biggest mistake was to chuck it away. Paul and Mary insist on having a bake to judge, and Iain ended up making the long lonely journey to the front of the tent carrying a sad-looking pedal bin. They who must be obeyed pointed out that they could still have judged his sponge and meringue. 'It got the better of you,' Mary gracefully suggested. 'It was just a moment in your life that you want to forget.' Iain couldn't help but agree.

DON'T! Serve anything shop-bought.

A helpful tip – never, ever, ever serve too much of something that you haven't crafted yourself.

Had Enwezor been given this warning, he might've been spared the crushing humiliation of Mary Berry's most terrifying death stare, back in 2014. 'I'm a bit of an amateur when it comes to decorating,' Enwezor forewarned while he fussed away during the Biscuit Week 3D-biscuit challenge. Amateur or not, it looked promising, with his edible rocket in cheery yellow fondant icing shaping up nicely. But there were sugary shockwaves at the judges' table.

'Did you make the fondant?' Paul enquired.

'No, I didn't,' Enwezor admitted, with trepidation.

Wordlessly, Mary communicated shock and disappointment, sending an arctic chill through the tent.

Remember too Brendan's 2012 Gingerbread Birdhouse in Biscuit Week:

'I'm somewhat disappointed we've got a breakfast cereal as the tiles,' sighed Mary, not happy that Brendan had created a birdhouse with an entire thatch of shop-bought Shredded Wheat. So if you don't want to be ripped to shreddies, make as much as you can yourself!

DON'T! Be precious.

You spend hours lovingly crafting that beautiful, delicate bake, but make sure you admire it before you serve it up to Paul Hollywood. With just one finger, that man will violate your buns, crush your custard tart or pulverise your petits fours. His 'digit of doom' won't spare your feelings as it dives in to investigate the intricacies of your bake.

There are four main functions of Paul's digit of doom:

1. Prod! Investigate the structure of a cake where a fork just won't do.

2. Squish! Homing in on raw dough like a heat-seeking missile....

3. Point! Didn't anybody tell you it was rude to point, Paul?

4. Tear! When one finger isn't enough, a five-pronged approach is called for.

MOST IMPORTANT 'DO'

Just bake the absolute best that you can – that's all you can really do to impress Paul and Mary.

YOUR BAKES FROM HOME

We've all had disasters in the kitchen, the bakers in the tent being no exception. We salute your valiant attempts at flying the baking flag, even if the end result wasn't quite Star Baker quality...

Better Luck Next Time!

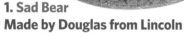

1. Sad Bear
Made by Douglas from Lincoln

Oh, dear! We can only presume this bear wasn't designed to appear quite as down in the dumps as he looks. We love the jaunty ribbon around the neck, though.

2. Cheesecake Meltdown
Made by Jan from London

This cheesecake didn't make it to the table. In certain situations, it's probably best just to admit defeat and hit the supermarket for a replacement. Best get some extra kitchen paper while you're there too!

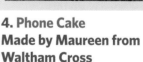

3. Red Velvet Bake Disaster
Made by Karen from Swansea

Well, it's red and it almost resembles a cake, so you're halfway there, Karen! We're sure Mary Berry would applaud you for your colouring efforts, even if your design skills could do with a bit of brushing up.

4. Phone Cake
Made by Maureen from Waltham Cross

A lovely colour, evenly distributed chocolate chips in the bake and, oh yes, a phone embedded in the mix. The world's first cake with 3G and texting capabilities!

5. Burnt Angel Cookies
Made by Elizabeth

It's the thought that counts. And a lot of thought has gone into these cookie creations, lovingly shaped into flying angels. It's just a shame that they were baked for roughly six hours longer than they should have been!

6. Hedgehog from Hell
Made by Sally from Rossendale

We never thought we'd be terrified by a cake, so this is a first. We're not sure what kind of hedgehogs you get where you come from, Sally, but this creature is the stuff of nightmares!

7. Brushy Bread
Made by Jo from Sheffield

Jo's bread bake was going so well, then she discovered where her pastry brush had got to. Oh, well – it's extra fibre!

C ombining a love of baking and a passion for *Bake Off*, these bakes show what happens when fans of the show recreate some of their favourite elements – whether finding inspiration in Mary, Paul, Mel and Sue, or just paying tribute to the *Bake Off* family. Here are some of our favourite fan-baked homages.

1. The Judging Table
Made by Margaret from Barton

There's so much we enjoy about this cake – the way Margaret has perfectly captured both judges' deep blue eyes, Mary's snazzy jacket and Paul's goatee, all so well observed. We're not sure exactly how much of this is edible, but, in a way, it would be a shame to spoil it!

Fan Bakes

2. GBBO Cupcakes
Made by Lottie from Sheffield

These chocolate mud cupcakes come with hand-drawn illustrations on edible rice paper of Mary, a particularly fierce-looking Paul, Mel and Sue – perfect if you're having a *Bake Off* party.

3. *Bake Off* Bread
Made by An from Belgium

She's such a big fan of the show that An has gone to the trouble of baking 22 individual spelt and oatmeal rolls spelling out its name, and they look delicious. (Top tip: make sure your spelling is up to scratch before attempting these.)

4. Iain Cake
Made by Tilly

It's not only the judges who get celebrated in sponge. This is an edible tribute to 2014's bearded baker, Iain. The icing accuracy is stunning, even down to the fact that Iain's bushy facial hair is a slightly different shade from the hair on his head. This is one bake we are not going to bin!

For more viewer bakes, or to send your own efforts to us, visit thegreatbritishbakeoff.co.uk/join-the-bake-off

Necessity is the mother of invention, and over the years the need to win *Bake Off* has brought forth all manner of gadgets and gizmos, contraptions and contrivances that the bakers have used to give them a cutting edge.

Here are the best of the inventions brought into the tent, with some suggestions for other possible uses of these widgets.

BAKE OFF'S GREAT INVENTORS

SIMON'S CUPCAKE HOLDER (2011)

The first truly impressive homemade invention to enter the tent came during Cake Week's Cupcake Challenge. Simon's multi-pronged contraption, precision-engineered from recycled lollipop sticks, might have looked more like a medieval instrument of torture, but once adorned with his Guinness and Chocolate Cupcakes, it resembled a bouquet of ornate roses.

JUDGES' VERDICT: 'It's different,' was Paul's reaction. We say different is good, Simon!

OTHER POSSIBLE USES: An exhibit in the Tower of London; the perfect gift for someone who loves lollipops; somewhere to hang your keys.

SMOOTH WOODEN FINISH DOESN'T CONDUCT HEAT, SO MIXTURE COOLS MORE QUICKLY

EASY-TO-GRIP HANDLE

WHEN FILLED, THE BRANDYSNAPS CREATE DAINTY '99' PETITS FOURS

CHRISTINE'S BRANDYSNAP CONE MOULD (2013)

When Christine told her husband, Rob, that she needed something cone-shaped for moulding her brandysnaps during Dessert Week, he came up with this handy wooden tool. Warm brandysnaps, fresh from the oven, are wrapped around it individually, and then cool into smart, strong cone shapes. Although it's a kitchen gadget infrequently needed (let's be honest – not many of us make brandysnap '99s' every day of the week), it will satisfy all of your moulded cone-related needs.

JUDGES' VERDICT: Mary was impressed with the cone and commended the ingenuity of Christine's husband. 'He should be mentioned in dispatches!' she beamed. She was equally impressed with the final result, saying it was 'very difficult' to make brandysnaps into cones.

OTHER POSSIBLE USES: Doorstop; dibber for planting seeds; device for Paul to use when poking about in bakes (thereby avoiding wear and tear on his finger).

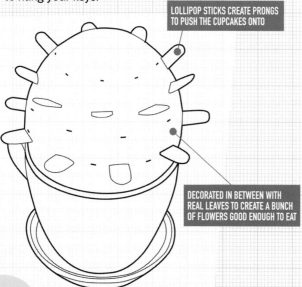

LOLLIPOP STICKS CREATE PRONGS TO PUSH THE CUPCAKES ONTO

DECORATED IN BETWEEN WITH REAL LEAVES TO CREATE A BUNCH OF FLOWERS GOOD ENOUGH TO EAT

NANCY'S CAKE GUILLOTINE (2014)

When Paul and Mary ask for a bake to be 'executed with precision', there's one gizmo that will do that quite literally. Nancy's cake guillotine was made by husband Tim under her close instruction. She came up with the invention in order to create 12 miniature Victoria sponge cakes of exactly the same size during the Final. The freshly baked cake is positioned, like a sponge Marie Antoinette, inside the contraption, and before you can say 'Let them eat cakes of a uniform size', the blade descends to make a perfect cut. Zing! Thud! (OK, maybe not the thud – Nancy's sponge was light as air.)

JUDGES' VERDICT: 'Your little gadget has worked really well; every one is exactly right,' a satisfied Mary declared.

OTHER POSSIBLE USES: Sausage cutter; cigar trimmer.

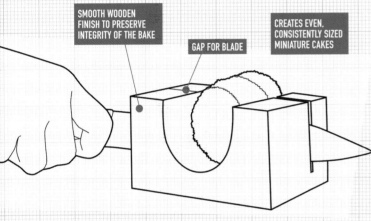

SMOOTH WOODEN FINISH TO PRESERVE INTEGRITY OF THE BAKE

GAP FOR BLADE

CREATES EVEN, CONSISTENTLY SIZED MINIATURE CAKES

NORMAN'S SUGAR BALL (2014)

With a reputation as Bake Off's inventor par excellence, Norman produced a range of clever gadgets, including a dowel rod gizmo for removing a cake from the tin, and a porcelain mini-skateboard to show off his Swiss Roll. His quirky take on a sieve featured in a blink-and-you-might-miss it moment. We all know how effective it can be to finish off a bake with a dusting of icing sugar. It's a classic look much loved by Norman, especially when he's making his Tarte au Citron, as he did in Pies and Tarts Week. A lesser baker might reach for the safe old sieve, but not Norman, who prefers what he describes as 'an old Scottish method'. A muslin cloth is fashioned into a bag for the icing sugar, and the simple addition of a standard golf ball transforms it into an effective dusting tool. Ta dah!

JUDGES' VERDICT: They never actually saw him use the invention, but it wouldn't have helped Norman if they had. The finished bake was not sprinkled with praise. 'I think it looks a mess,' Paul told Norman.

OTHER POSSIBLE USES: Can be tied to a tree to scare squirrels away; 'sugar slinging', which involves whirling the bag around the head and releasing the golf ball and sugar at speed (will be included in the 2016 Olympics if Norman has his way).

MUSLIN CLOTH ENSURES EVEN DISTRIBUTION OF SUGAR

GOLF BALL CREATES MOVEMENT INSIDE THE BAG

SHAKE TO ACTIVATE!

RICHARD'S ÉCLAIR STAIRS (2014)

When it came to tackling Pastry Week, Richard the builder couldn't quite leave his day job behind. He decided that plates and cake stands simply weren't good enough to display his éclairs to their best advantage, so he crafted a beautiful set of wooden stairs for the purpose. Solving the age-old conundrum of choux storage, this structure is an inventive yet simple way to draw attention to your wonderful bakes.

JUDGES' VERDICT: They didn't even mention it! Bit rude. They were too busy talking about the éclairs to comment on the food furniture Richard had crafted. What is this, a baking contest or something?

OTHER POSSIBLE USES: Richard himself revealed that his contraption also doubles as a handy staircase for chickens (just make sure you give it a good scrub if you intend to use it for pastry again); also good for displaying your 'Many Faces of Paul Hollywood' limited edition porcelain plate collection.

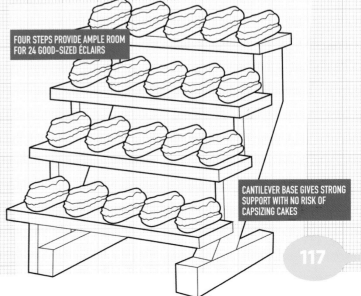

FOUR STEPS PROVIDE AMPLE ROOM FOR 24 GOOD-SIZED ÉCLAIRS

CANTILEVER BASE GIVES STRONG SUPPORT WITH NO RISK OF CAPSIZING CAKES

AT HOME *With* TAMAL

What got you into baking?

My sister got me into it. She'd make little cakes and things like crumbles. Then, while at university, I began attempting more complicated stuff, like macarons.

You made your sister's wedding cake – what was it like?

It was a traditional fruit cake, three tiers. It had candystripe piping and flowers on top. It did all go to plan, but I had loads of helpful advice from the ladies running the cake shop round the corner.

Tell us about your earliest food memory.

Having Christmas dinner with my family. Even though we're not Christian, Christmas was always a big deal and the table would be full of food. One year Mum forgot to serve the roast potatoes and no one noticed because the table was so full already.

What's your guilty food pleasure?

I'd have to say burgers. I like them with everything on, mature cheese, pickles, the works.

If you could invite anyone past or present around for tea, who would it be and what would you bake?

Leonardo da Vinci. I'd try and make him some ornate patisserie that we could have over tea, and then I'd get him to give me some drawing lessons.

If you could bake only one thing, what would it be?

I really love making croissants. I like the sort of bakes that allow you to take your time, and croissants are things you just can't rush.

When you're not baking, how do you relax?

I like drawing. I take a sketchbook everywhere with me now, and I use it for baking ideas too.

Who do you like to bake for?

For my family – they get quite excited about it. My ideal weekend would end with us having Sunday tea with freshly made scones. Lately I've also been baking for my colleagues at work too.

Can baking be a form of therapy?

It can be for me. Medicine is not a particularly creative job, but baking and drawing let me show my creative side.

What are your five favourite bakes?

Sourdough, baked cheesecake, mango macarons, crème brûlée and croissants.

What's your worst baking disaster?

Once I tried to make this cranberry toffee stuff as a Christmas experiment. It was bubbling away on the stove, so I nipped out for, at most, 90 seconds. When I came back there was black smoke everywhere, and the smoke alarm was going off. My parents were livid and wouldn't let me make it again. I made a batch the following year, though.

What's the most surprising, unusual or interesting thing in your cupboard?

Dried hibiscus flowers, which I bought for a bake and have never used, but I do want to as they were quite expensive.

What's your favourite kitchen gadget?

A digital kitchen thermometer, which I bought initially for cooking fudges and caramels, but that I now use instead of a skewer for testing cakes. Perhaps it's because of my medical background – I'm used to having a number rather than relying on a gooey skewer.

Describe your kitchen at home.

The oven's all electric, so the hobs are horrendous as they stay hot for ages. We've burnt loads of things on them, like plastic utensils and tea towels. Just looking around, there's a lot of my stuff everywhere – every space has something on it.

What's your favourite ingredient to work with?

Lately it's been date molasses. I've been putting it in biscuits and things.

Do you keep a recipe notebook?

Yes, I started doing that a year and a half ago. If I've had something nice in a restaurant or café, or I get an idea, I'll scribble it all down.

What's your party trick?

I can open a bottle of wine using a shoe! Something like a trainer works best. You put the wine in the shoe, whack it against a hard surface and it gradually eases the cork out. I only do this when there's no corkscrew available!

Tell us one thing about yourself that will surprise us.

I went cage-diving with great white sharks a few years ago, one of my life ambitions.

What did it feel like when you found out you'd been selected for *Bake Off* 2015?

It was pretty amazing. Even after they said the words, it still didn't feel real. On the first day I fully expected someone with a clipboard to ask me to leave. It didn't become real until we actually got into the tent and started to do that first bake.

What's your favourite *Bake Off* moment from a previous series?

In Series Five, those biscuit scenes, particularly Luis' and Richard's, were so imaginative and inspiring.

Who's your favourite past baker and why?

Mary-Anne from Series Two. She was doing stuff then like opera cake and entremet that would be Showstoppers and Technicals in later series.

AT HOME
With
UGNE

What got you into baking?

It comes from my childhood, my mum and and my grandma both spent a lot of time in the kitchen. In school holidays we'd visit my grandparents, and the house would always smell amazing. In Lithuania it was traditional bakes like apple pies, plum pies. You used whatever you grew in your garden.

Tell us about your earliest food memory.

We used to live in the city, then my parents moved out and built a house in the countryside. My grandma would make these amazing butter cookies called *sviestiniai sausainiai*, which involved pushing the dough through a mould. They're buttery and crumbly, similar to shortbread. All Lithuanian baking is quite basic and simple; we didn't use lots of expensive spices. The flavour came from the fruit and vegetables you grew in your garden. It's quite rustic.

What's your guilty food pleasure?

I love French food, lots of butter and great pastry, and as a couple, we do like eating out. At home, it's chocolate that's my guilty pleasure.

If you could invite anyone past or present around for tea, who would it be and what would you bake?

I'd have two guests: Mich Turner, as she's my cake-making idol, and Arnold Schwarzenegger, for his extraordinary achievements in fitness, politics and the movie industry. I'd serve a pot of Earl Grey, and chocolate fondant with raspberry coulis.

If you could bake only one thing, what would it be?

Bread, because you can vary the flavours of it so much and make so many different types. When I was pregnant, I'd bake bread every day.

When you're not baking, how do you relax?

Family time is important and we spend a lot of time together. I like to go out for a stroll, especially along the river in London after a lunch with family.

Who do you like to bake for?

Family and friends – they're the judging panel of what I do! They're always asking me to make various things.

What are your five favourite bakes?

Chocolate fondant, *trupininis pyragas* – a Lithuanian crumble pie with blackberries, any kind of chocolate cake, a traditional honey cake called *medutis*, and cheese curd doughnuts.

What's your worst baking disaster?

I like to experiment in the kitchen, so disasters are inevitable! I tried a new cake recipe recently, which completely flopped and went in the bin. I tried to tweak the flavourings a bit, and yep, it didn't work. I wouldn't say it was inedible, but it wasn't the best cake I've ever made.

What's the most surprising, unusual or interesting thing in your cupboard?

Lavender. It's always in my cupboard because I like it as a flavour, particularly when combined with hazelnuts. If I make chocolate hazelnut cake, I have special lavender buds that I grind and put in the batter to give a nice flavour. It's also great with chocolate ganache. You can put in too much, however, as it's very strong.

What's your favourite kitchen gadget?

My stand mixer. It really is my kitchen helper. I also like my little pastry cutters. All the equipment I have gives good results if used right, but I would love to have more!

Describe your kitchen at home?

My kitchen is not that big and I don't have a lot of workspace. It's kind of basic; I don't even have a microwave. All my gadgets are tucked away in cupboards. I spend a lot of time here, sometimes a whole weekend. I'm a working woman too, so to do that is quite a lot. If we move, I want a bigger kitchen!

What's your favourite ingredient to work with?

Chocolate. It's so versatile. You can use it to make pie fillings, cakes, truffles. It also tastes amazing and there are so many different varieties. Yeast is good too, though.

Do you keep a recipe notebook?

Yes, I've always had my scribbles. It's more like a scrapbook with notes and tips. I also have a separate folder of recipes, which is separated into sections, such as cakes and cookies.

Tell us one thing about yourself that will surprise us.

I used to ride horses. I also used to play basketball and run marathons at national level in Lithuania. Growing up, I wasn't girly at all. I was fixing cars with Dad. I'm actually better at DIY than my other half is.

You're also a keen bodybuilder – that's quite a combination with baking.

Baking is from my childhood; it's in my heart and it's what I remember. Sports became part of my life in high school. I always was a fitness fanatic, and my other half competed in bodybuilding competitions at national level, so I wanted to see if I could push myself to those limits. But if I had to choose, I'd choose baking. You can be fit and bake, you don't need to be greedy eating the cakes.

What did it feel like when you found out you'd been selected for *Bake Off* 2015?

The producer heard a lot of squeaking on the phone! It was an amazing feeling. I wanted to be on the show for years but I'd never applied.

How did you prepare for *Bake Off*?

I didn't panic – I made a list of the techniques and recipes I knew I would need to improve on, then I sat down and learnt them. Little details are my weakness. I'm fairly rustic. I need to be more refined.

What's your favourite *Bake Off* moment from a previous series?

All the Technicals are so exciting. *Bake Off* is for amateur bakers, and they learn through the series. That's why I love it so much. And I love Mel and Sue - they're so hilarious. My favourite bake would be the squirrel cake Frances made.

Who's your favourite past baker and why?

Frances. I loved Kimberley too. She has a feisty personality. But Frances is a deserving winner.

BAKEBATS

Can you decipher these codes to reveal the names of the bakes?

Example: ▢ + [Mary] / [P] + [eye] = Blueberry pie

▼▼▼▼▼▼▼▼▼▼▼

1 [moon] + [Y] + [pan] = ▢▢▢▢▢▢▢

2 [tree] + [bird] / [tea] + [easel] = ▢▢▢▢▢▢▢▢ / ▢▢▢▢

3 [crocodile] + **M** + [Bush] = ▢▢▢▢▢▢▢▢▢▢▢▢

4 [Swiss flag] / [roll] = ▢▢▢▢▢ / ▢▢▢▢

5 [tear] + [Cheryl] + [Mel] = ▢▢▢▢▢▢▢▢

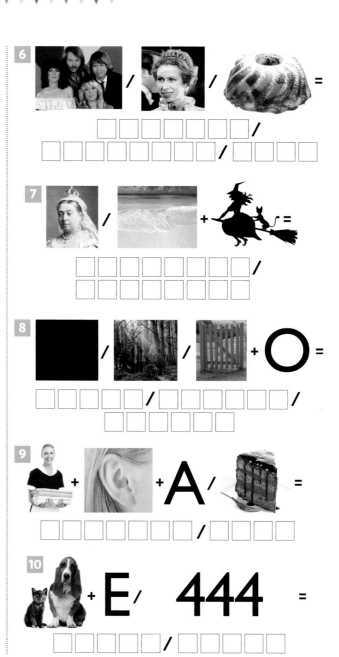

6 [ABBA] / [Princess Anne] / [bundt] = ▢▢▢▢▢ / ▢▢▢▢▢▢▢ / ▢▢▢▢

7 [Queen Victoria] / [sea] + [witch] = ▢▢▢▢▢▢▢▢▢ / ▢▢▢▢▢▢▢▢

8 ▢ / [wood] / [gate] + **O** = ▢▢▢▢ / ▢▢▢▢▢▢▢ / ▢▢▢▢▢

9 [book/ear] + [ear] + **A** / [cake] = ▢▢▢▢▢▢▢ / ▢▢▢▢

10 [basset hound] + **E** / **444** = ▢▢▢▢▢ / ▢▢▢▢▢▢

Answers on page 124

122

WORDSEARCH

There are 80 Bake Off and baking-related words hidden in this jumble of letters. Can you find every one of them?

▼ ▼ ▼ ▼ ▼ ▼ ▼ ▼ ▼ ▼ ▼ ▼ ▼ ▼ ▼

B	U	T	E	N	B	Z	W	E	L	L	I	N	G	T	O	N	I	S	L
A	R	C	U	B	Y	A	C	C	L	E	C	U	S	L	N	A	W	T	D
T	A	E	M	R	A	M	Y	D	T	R	I	F	L	E	G	L	E	U	O
T	R	E	A	F	E	T	L	W	S	A	N	D	X	N	I	U	L	D	U
M	A	M	A	D	L	D	T	L	P	U	G	F	I	L	O	M	E	E	G
U	N	T	K	Q	S	D	R	E	O	R	W	K	T	R	A	R	T	R	H
F	D	R	B	U	A	E	G	I	N	R	A	N	G	S	M	O	L	S	N
F	Y	P	Y	E	E	S	B	N	G	B	L	I	F	C	U	L	M	U	U
I	B	A	E	J	L	S	E	G	E	P	E	C	L	H	S	T	A	R	T
N	D	P	A	U	L	E	O	T	H	U	G	R	H	I	T	H	C	E	P
D	C	U	S	T	A	R	D	R	A	B	E	W	G	C	A	C	A	R	P
R	A	S	T	T	E	T	F	L	E	P	B	R	E	H	F	L	R	O	A
E	K	L	E	A	I	N	O	N	P	G	R	U	J	T	F	Q	O	O	P
O	E	Q	U	C	E	M	T	O	I	N	G	E	A	T	I	L	N	Q	E
M	U	L	I	S	I	N	T	N	E	N	T	E	N	O	L	A	O	P	F
A	E	W	O	W	E	S	E	M	I	Y	E	A	S	R	D	O	A	A	F
L	S	Q	O	C	W	M	B	R	F	F	N	N	I	T	L	C	D	S	F
B	C	C	R	O	Q	U	E	M	B	O	U	C	H	E	C	L	U	T	S
Q	U	E	H	I	N	M	I	N	G	B	R	U	E	L	D	O	R	R	T
T	E	S	U	E	S	O	E	S	T	R	U	D	E	L	L	Y	O	Y	C

CLUES

The words run left to right, downwards or diagonally. There are:

Three 3-letter words
Eight 4-letter words

Three 5-letter words
Five 6-letter words
Four 7-letter words
Two 8-letter words

Two 10-letter words
One 11-letter word
One 12-letter word
One 13-letter word

ANSWERS

GREAT BIG BAKE OFF QUIZ
Round One

1c. 2b. 3a. 4c. 5b. 6c. 7b. 8d. 9a. 10d. 11d. 12b. 13a. 14 Rob (2011). 15 James (2012). 16 Frances (2013). 17 Charlotte Royal (baked by Beca, 2013). 18 Swedish Princess Cake (baked by Nancy, 2014). 19 Schichttorte (baked by Luis, 2014). 20 Iced Fingers (baked by Holly, 2011). 21 Crème Caramel (baked by Brendan, 2012). 22b. 23a. 25a.

Your score: ____/25

Round Two

1 Martha (2014). 2 Diana (2014). 3d. 4c. 5c. 6b. 7c. 8c. 9b. 10b. 11 Queen of Puddings (baked by Brendan, 2012). 12 Fraisier Cake (baked by James, 2012). 13 Classic French Tuiles (baked by Christine, 2013). 14 Lemon Soufflé (baked by Miranda, 2010). 15 Battenberg Cake (baked by Holly, 2011). 16c. 17d. 18b. 19c. 20d. 21 Ben (2011). 22 Natasha (2012). 23 Urvashi (2011). 24 Ali (2013). 25 Enwezor (2014).

Your score: ____/25

Round Three

1 c. 2 a. 3 a. 4 a. 5 c. 6 a. 7 Kate (2014). 8 Howard (2013). 9 Ruby (2013). 10 Richard (2014). 11 Iain (2014). 12 c. 13 b. 14 c. 15 b. 16 d. 17 b. 18 a. 19 b. 20 b. 21 d. 22 d. 23 James. 24 Diana. 25 Jordan.

Your score: ____/25

Round Four

1 c. 2 a. 3 a. 4 a. 5 d. 6 Chocolate Roulade baked by Jo, 2011). 7 Rum Baba (baked by Sarah-Jane, 2012). 8 Chocolate Teacakes (baked by James, 2012). 9 Dacquoise (baked by Ruby, 2013). 10 Florentines (baked by Richard, 2014). 11 d. 12 d. 13 c. 14 a. 15 c. 16 b. 17 d. 18 b. 19 b. 20 b. 21. Victoria (2012). 22. Cathryn (2012). 23. Toby (2013). 24. Mark (2013). 25. Annetha (2010).

Your score: ____/25

Add up your grand total and see how baking brainy you are!

____/100

How did you do?

80–100	Star Baker!
60–79	Tasty, but not quite perfect
40–59	A bit pale and undercooked
20–39	Didn't rise to the challenge
10–19	Soggy bottom
1–9	Cake wreck!

CROSSWORD SOLUTION

B	A	P	S		B	U	N	S			T	A	R	T	E
	M		I	R		K		I							S
B	E	E	F	W	E	L	L	I	N	G	T	O	N	S	
	R		T	A		N		H		H				E	
T	I	N	S		D	U	O	S		T		T	A	T	I	N
	C			S		R		S	M			M		C	
G	A	D	G	E	T		E	V	E	N	B	A	K	E	
	L		I		G		R		E					
F	O	C	A	C	C	I	A		V	E	R	O	N	A	
L		Z	K	N		E		O					
A	N	G	E	L		F	O	O	D		C	A	K	E	
V			I	R		C		H		N	
O	V	E	N	T	H	E	R	M	O	M	E	T	E	R	
U			R	S		L		F		A	
R	A	N	G	E		H	A	N	D		S	O	D	A	

BAKEBATS

1. Mars + Y + pan = Marzipan
2. Tree + gull + tea + art = Treacle tart
3. Croc + M + Bush = Croquembouche
4. Swiss + roll = Swiss roll
5. Tear + Amy (Childs) + Sue = Tiramisu
6. Abba + princess + cake = Swedish princess cake
7. Victoria + sand + witch = Victoria sandwich
8. Black + forest + gate + O = Black Forest gateau
9. Maid + ear + A + cake = Madeira cake
10. Pet + E + fours = Petits fours

WORDSEARCH

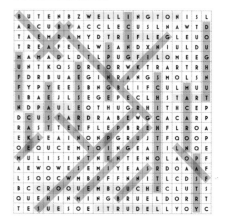

Three-letter words
Mel / Pie / Sue

Four-letter words
Buns / Cake / Filo / Loaf Mary / Paul / Tart / Tent

Five-letter words
Bread / Icing / Yeast

Six-letter words
Baking / Muffin / Pastry / Sponge / Trifle

Seven-letter words
Custard / Dessert / Macaron / Strudel

Eight-letter words
Doughnut / Meringue

Ten-letter words
Battenberg / Wellington

Eleven-letter words
Showstopper

Twelve-letter words
Schichttorte

Thirteen-letter words
Croquembouche